wagamama

your way

wagamama

your way

fresh flexible recipes for body + mind

contents

foreword

In my 25 years of cooking, there is one thing that I can wholeheartedly say is true…the experience of creating a meal and enjoying it with mates is good for the mind, the body and, most importantly, the soul.

Now, when it comes to creating soulful food to share, you cannot beat modern Asian cuisine. Simple combinations of freshness, textures and flavours can result in the most soulful of bowlfuls. Simple combinations of the freshest Asian flavours. That's what this book is about.

Some people like to follow recipes exactly and others like to freestyle, changing and customising along the way. Whichever kind of cook you are, I've designed the recipes in this book to inspire you to cook wagamama, your way.

Recipes that range from fast and easy, to more complex. From salads and noodle bowls, to stir-fries and sweet things. There are breakfasts, light bites, lunches and suppers. This book has a bowl for everyone. Plus, for our plant-based people, in the recipes that aren't already vegetarian or vegan, you'll find simple swaps to make them so.

Printed together, these pages become a recipe in itself. A recipe for modern nourishment. Your reason to roll up your sleeves, get stuck in and cook up wagamama, your way.

Happy cooking and happy eating.

Steve Mangleshot

wagamama

わがまま

In Japanese, wagamama means naughty child. Wilful, playful and restless – to be wagamama is to be driven by a constant curiosity.

Eager to try new things and explore new places…not a bad attitude for a cook.

wagamama your way

from bowl to soul since 1992

In 1992, the doors to our first restaurant in London flew open and wagamama welcomed people from all walks of life inside.

Strangers sitting side by side on long benches, slurping ramen and sharing a moment of pause from modern life.

Our bowls, inspired by Japanese noodle bars and an unwavering belief in the power of positive eating and positive living, have continued to bring people together ever since.

And whilst today's menu looks a little different and a lot larger to the one served in 1992 (thanks to our ever-growing vegan menu), we've stayed true to our beliefs, and we won't change for anyone.

We're passionate about treading softly on the earth. About championing plant-based alternatives. About supporting and shining a light on mental health issues, especially for young people. And about being an active ally for diversity and inclusion.

Side by side. All on one bench. A safe sanctuary, from bowl to soul.

from our way to your way

As lifelong students of Asian cuisine, we at wagamama are forever inspired by the fiercely fresh flavours of the East. Visits to Japan, China, Thailand and beyond have shaped the menus you see on the wagamama benches today. From markets to restaurants. Farmers to food stalls. Steamy noodle bars to street side queues.

Fresh thinking and fresher ingredients are the backbones of our food philosophy, resulting in soul-warming bowls to nourish the body and mind.

When it comes to food, we're restless, continuously looking to sharpen our skills, refine our recipes and find fresh new flavours.

We hope this book inspires you to do the same. To take some of our favourites and add your own twist. To make wagamama – your way.

fresh flexibility

There's no one way to wagamama. In fact, there are hundreds.

Just like our menu, this book has a bowl for everyone and, just like in our restaurants, you can modify the dishes to meet your needs. Add extra sauce. Use less spice. Swap white rice for brown rice or proteins for plant-based.

This swappable spirit has been carried through wagamama your way…

If a dish isn't vegan or vegetarian already, we've included a hack that means you can make it so. If it's non-gluten you need, we've indicated how some recipes can be made gluten-free.

Look out for the coloured dots on each recipe page which let you know if the dish is already vegan, vegetarian or gluten-free. Plus, look out for the hacks on the page which can help make the dish meet your dietary needs.

● vegan

● vegetarian

● gluten-free

ingredients

These are some of our favourite ingredients that we use on a daily basis in our wagamama kitchens.

chilli oil / chilli flakes
Often used simply to add heat to a sauce or finished dish.

chilli paste
A simple crushed chilli paste is perfect for adding a spike of heat to any dish or sauce and there are many different kinds. We like Korean 'gochujang', which is sweet, spicy and fermented.

citrus ponzu
Traditionally a yuzu lemon-based Japanese condiment made with soy and mirin.
Ingredient swap | juice of a lemon or lime, with a dash of white vinegar, a tablespoon of soy sauce and a teaspoon of honey. The flavour should be tart, so taste and adjust as necessary.

coconut milk
This is the liquid that has been extracted from coconut flesh and is used as a base in many of our curry recipes.

crispy fried onions
These bring a lovely crunchy texture and deep, savoury flavour to many Asian dishes.

edamame
Edamame are young soya beans, most often still in their pod. They can also be found, podded, in the frozen aisles of most large supermarkets.
Ingredient swap | garden peas or broad beans.

fish sauce
Or 'nam pla' is a liquid extracted from salted and fermented fish. It is a light golden-brown colour and has a pungent, salty taste, which is used to add depth to dishes and enhance the umami flavours.

galangal
From the same family as ginger, galangal has a dry, peppery and spicy flavour. It can be found as a paste or dry form in many supermarkets.
Ingredient swap | can be substituted with ginger, but there are slight flavour differences.

kewpie mayonnaise
This Japanese-style mayonnaise is richer than regular mayonnaise as it contains more egg yolk. It also uses mild vegetable oil, rice vinegar instead of white vinegar and contains additional seasoning, so the taste is quite a contrast.

kimchee
A classic Korean side dish which is made by fermenting cabbage and carrots in a flavoursome sauce, pungent with garlic and spice. It is widely available in supermarkets, but we've also created a recipe so you can make your own (see page 179).

menma
Menma is a Japanese condiment made from sun-dried fermented bamboo shoots. We use menma in many of our ramen recipes.
Ingredient swap | tinned bamboo shoots.

miso paste
A Japanese paste traditionally made from fermented soya beans and some sort of grain, such as rice or barley, and more recently many other ingredient varieties. We mainly use white miso, which is made with rice. White miso has a sweet, light and delicate flavour, which adds a rich umami taste to marinades, sauces and stocks.
Ingredient swap | a mix of light soy, sugar and fish sauce.

mooli
Mooli or 'daikon' is a mild-flavoured radish, native to South-east Asia. In terms of appearance, this vegetable resembles a large, white carrot.
Ingredient swap | salad radish.

noodles
Long, thin, stretched pieces of dough that are the perfect addition or centrepiece of many Asian dishes.
udon noodles | the 'comfort food' of all noodles – a thick, chewy wheat noodle.
glass bean noodles | extremely thin noodles traditionally made out of mung beans.
rice noodles | quite simply, noodles made from cooked rice. Flat, long and thin.
ramen noodles | long, curly noodles usually made from egg.

oyster sauce
This is a thick brown sauce made from oysters cooked down with soy sauce and seasoning.

panko breadcrumbs
Breadcrumbs with a light, flaky texture. These are generally used in Japanese cooking as a coating for fried or baked food.

pickled ginger
Widely available and usually served with sushi. We also like to use this fresh, sweet and peppery garnish to finish off many of our stir-fry dishes.

rice
A staple food of Asian cuisine and the most consumed grain in the world, even more than wheat.
short grain rice | a more starchy rice with a shorter grain. Traditionally used to make sushi/sticky rice.
jasmine/long grain rice | due to the longer grain, this rice is less starchy.
brown rice | any rice that is not polished is 'brown rice'. The polishing process removes the bran layer. You can get various lengths of brown rice as you can with white rice.

rice vinegar
This is also referred to as rice wine vinegar. It is made from fermented rice and has a slightly sweet flavour that is milder and less acidic than distilled vinegar.

sesame oil
Derived from sesame seeds, this oil has a distinct fragrant flavour and complements most Asian dishes.

shichimi
Sometimes also referred to as 'seven spice pepper', this is
a mix of chilli pepper, black pepper, dried orange peel,
sesame seeds, poppy seeds, nori seaweed and hemp
seeds. It adds a kick of flavour to many noodle stir-fry
dishes and is widely available in Asian supermarkets.
ingredient swap | chilli flakes.

shiitake mushrooms
Native to East Asia, these mushrooms (particularly
the dried variety) are rich in flavour and their meaty taste
means they work very well in vegetarian stocks and
broths. Fresh and dried shiitake are available in most
large supermarkets.
Ingredient swap | for a fresh shiitake replacement, most
mushrooms work well, including chestnut or button. For
a dried shiitake replacement, dried porcini will work well.

soy sauce
There are two main types; a light version that is most
commonly used in cooking or to season food and a dark
soy sauce that is stronger in colour and far saltier in taste.

sriracha
This South-east Asian hot sauce is made from a paste of
chilli peppers, distilled vinegar, garlic, sugar and salt, and is
widely available.

tamari
This is the Japanese version of soy sauce and contains
no wheat, which makes it the perfect soy sauce substitute
for use in gluten-free dishes.

tempeh
Originating in Indonesia, tempeh is made from fermented
soy beans. It is a great vegan meat replacement that is
high in protein, and research shows it is great for the gut.

tempura
A light batter widely used in Japanese cuisine to coat meat,
seafood or vegetables.

teriyaki sauce
A versatile sauce – it makes a great marinade for
grilled meats, oily fish and vegetables, can be used to
finish a dish and also works well as a sweet and salty
dipping sauce.

tofu
Also known as bean curd, it is made by coagulating soy
milk and then pressing it. The length of the press determines
the type of tofu you make.
silken tofu | as the name suggests, this has a softer
consistency than regular tofu and will fall apart if not
handled carefully. This is most commonly used in
traditional miso soup.
firm tofu | this tofu is created by using a harder press to
give a firmer texture. It is easier to use and is more suited
to the Western palate.

wakame
This edible seaweed originates from Japan. The flavour
is subtle with a hint of sweetness.
ingredient hack | dried nori sheets can be found in
most supermarkets.

fast
+
easy

Flipped from the teppan or hot off the wok – this chapter is inspired by the street food of Japan, where a bowl full of soul is created in minutes and served from a stall, straight to your hands for maximum freshness and enjoyment.

These recipes may seem simple but they don't skimp on flavour, and easy swaps mean you can enjoy them your way. Switch proteins for plant-based or use our cook at home range to save time.

Start the day with okonomyaki, wrap lunch up inside a roti, or enjoy our most iconic dish between two slices of bread. Even on your busiest days, these snackable staples make nourishment easy.

buckwheat + chia seed granola

Gluten-free granola with a wagamama twist.

makes roughly 200g (7oz)

120g (4½oz) buckwheat
a handful of green pumpkin seeds
2 handfuls of coconut flakes
a handful of chia seeds
a handful of goji berries
a handful of dried cranberries
1 teaspoon ground ginger
1 teaspoon ground cinnamon
2 tablespoons virgin coconut oil
4 tablespoons agave syrup

Preheat the oven to 160°C/325°F/gas mark 3.

Measure all the dry ingredients into a large bowl. Add the coconut oil and agave syrup and mix well until all the ingredients are nicely coated.

Line a large baking tray with greaseproof paper and spread the mixture on top. Bake in the oven for 10 minutes, then take out, mix well and return to the oven for a final 10 minutes.

Allow to cool for 45 minutes, until cold, before transferring to an airtight container.

✷ **Why not make this up in bulk and store in an airtight jar so you can use as you please throughout the week? It's great with yogurt, milk or even as a mid-afternoon snack.**

crunchy granola bowl with raspberry compote

serves 1

60ml (2½fl oz) coconut yogurt
50g (2oz) buckwheat granola
2 tablespoons raspberry compote or yuzu
    marmalade
a handful of pomegranate seeds

Place your yogurt, granola and compote or marmalade in a bowl and serve garnished with pomegranate seeds. Enjoy!

raspberry compote

makes 200g (7oz)

50g (2oz) sugar
200g (7oz) raspberries (fresh
    or frozen)
½ lime

Place a heavy-bottomed pan over a low heat, add the sugar along with half the raspberries and cook until the sugar dissolves, stirring occasionally.

Squeeze half a lime into the pan and cook for a further minute.

Take off the heat, stir through the remaining raspberries and set aside to cool.

Transfer to a container and refrigerate.

yuzu marmalade

makes 600g (1lb 5oz)

500g (1lb 2oz) vegan orange
    marmalade
100ml (3½fl oz) yuzu juice

Place the vegan marmalade and yuzu juice in a saucepan over a low heat and stir until combined.

Cool and decant into a dry, airtight container. Refrigerate and use when needed.

✳ **If you don't want to make this much, why not halve or quarter the ingredients?**

overnight oats

Prepare the night before for
a perfect start to your day.

serves 2

100g (3½fl oz) gluten-free rolled oats
1 tablespoon chia seeds
250ml (8fl oz) milk of your choice
3 tablespoons raspberry compote or
    yuzu marmalade (see page 27)
a handful of pomegranate seeds

Place the oats and chia seeds in a bowl, add enough milk to just cover the oats, then transfer to the fridge and leave overnight.

Remove from the fridge and serve in bowls with raspberry compote or yuzu marmalade.

Garnish with pomegranate seeds and enjoy.

✴ **Use any non-dairy milk to make this dish vegan. If you want to make the oat consistency a bit thicker, why not use half yogurt, half milk.**

yasai okonomiyaki

serves 2

60ml (2½fl oz) vegetable oil
50g (2oz) Savoy cabbage, finely sliced
50g (2oz) mixed mushrooms (oyster, chestnut, white), sliced
1 red pepper, sliced
½ leek, trimmed and roughly sliced
50g (2oz) asparagus, sliced
1 small red onion, sliced
salt and freshly ground black pepper

for the batter
100g (3½oz) plain flour
1 teaspoon bicarbonate of soda
50ml (2fl oz) vegetable oil
120ml (4fl oz) water

to serve
vegan mayonnaise, for drizzling
2 tablespoons amai (see page 176), for drizzling
1 sheet nori seaweed, finely sliced
1 spring onion, finely chopped
3 sprigs of coriander, leaves picked

First make the batter: sift the flour and bicarbonate of soda into a mixing bowl. In a separate bowl, mix the oil and water together and then slowly add this to the flour, whisking all the time to ensure there are no lumps.

Place a frying pan over a medium heat, add the oil and stir-fry the cut veg until the mushrooms are cooked. Season with salt and pepper to taste.

Add the batter to the pan of veg and, once it seems to be set, use a spatula to carefully flip the pancake and brown the other side.

When cooked, transfer the pancake to a serving plate. Drizzle over the vegan mayo and amai sauce in a zig-zag and garnish with the nori, spring onion and coriander.

✴ Why not use our off-the-shelf pad Thai sauce if you don't want to make the amai sauce?

✴ The authentic drizzle for an okonomiyaki is okonomi sauce, which you can enjoy if you are not vegan or vegetarian.

apple + goji berry soufflé pancakes

Perfect for breakfast, lunch or even dinner, these are light and fluffy pancakes with delicious sweet additions.

serves 2

20g (¾oz) goji berries
2 apples
30g (1oz) butter, at room temperature
3 free-range eggs, separated
50g (2oz) caster sugar
80g (3oz) self-raising flour
1 teaspoon baking powder
a pinch of salt
½ teaspoon lemon juice
10ml (2 teaspoons) vegetable oil
4 tablespoons agave syrup

Soak the goji berries in water for about 10 minutes, then drain off the water and set aside.

Peel and core one of the apples, then coarsely grate into a bowl. Slice the other apple into thin pieces.

Warm the butter in the microwave until just melted, and whisk with the egg yolks and half the caster sugar until frothy. Sift in the flour, baking powder and a pinch of salt and stir to make a smooth batter.

In a separate bowl, add the remaining caster sugar, egg whites and lemon juice and whisk until the egg whites hold their shape and are stiff and glossy. Next, fold the batter into the whites, together with the grated apple and goji berries.

Lightly oil a frying pan (with a lid) and place on a very low heat. When warm, scoop 4 dollops of batter into the pan to make 4 pancakes, then cover and cook for 3–4 minutes until they start bubbling on the surface. Use a spatula to gently flip the pancakes and cook for another 3 minutes.

To serve, arrange the pancakes onto a sharing plate with a few slices of apple, and drizzle with agave syrup.

katsu stack

A perfect way to start your day in wagamama style.

serves 2

2 Cumberland sausages

2 back bacon rashers, diced into small chunks

3 free-range eggs

10g (¼oz) plain flour

50g (2oz) panko breadcrumbs

100ml (3½oz) vegetable oil, for deep-frying

a drop of vinegar

40g (1½oz) baby spinach

20ml (⅔fl oz) sriracha sauce

20ml (⅔fl oz) Japanese kewpie mayonnaise

Squeeze all the sausage meat out from the skin into a bowl and mix together with the diced bacon. Divide into four servings and shape into small burger patties.

Crack one egg into a wide, shallow bowl and lightly beat it. Place the flour and panko breadcrumbs in two separate similar bowls. Roll each patty first in flour, then in egg and finally in breadcrumbs – this is your sausage katsu.

Take a deep pan, add the oil and, when hot, deep-fry the sausage katsu until golden brown. Remove with a slotted spoon and transfer to a plate lined with kitchen paper to soak up the excess oil. Keep warm.

Bring a pan of water to a simmer, add a drop of vinegar and swirl the water with a chopstick. Crack the two remaining eggs into the water and poach for 3–4 minutes – we prefer the yolk to still be a bit runny. Lift each egg out with a slotted spoon and drain on kitchen paper.

Divide the spinach between the plates, arrange the sausage katsus one on top of the other and drizzle with sriracha sauce.

Carefully place a poached egg on the top of each stack, drizzle with Japanese mayonnaise and serve.

✷ **To make this dish vegetarian you could leave out the bacon and use veggie sausages for your patties.**

vegetable yakitori

A vegan version of a typical Japanese street food – served on skewers.

serves 2

3 tablespoons yakitori sauce (see page 177)
2 king oyster mushrooms, diced into 2.5cm (1 in) pieces
2 spring onions, topped, tailed and diced
1 tablespoon vegetable oil
½ teaspoon shichimi

First prepare your yakitori sauce, following the instructions on page 177.

Thread the vegetables onto eight wooden skewers, alternating the mushroom and onion as you go.

Place a ridged griddle pan over a high heat and add the oil. When hot, place the skewers in the pan and cook for 30 seconds, then turn over and cook for about 10 seconds before reducing the heat. This will give you the bar marks on the vegetables. Continue cooking until all the vegetables are nicely caramelised.

Add a third of the sauce, turn the skewers, then add another third of the sauce and turn off the heat.

Transfer the skewers to a serving plate, drizzle with the remaining yakitori sauce and sprinkle with shichimi.

Because toast doesn't have to be boring.

avocado + scrambled tofu on toast

serves 2

1 large avocado, peeled and cut into 1cm (½in) chunks
1 large tomato, cut into 1cm (½in) chunks
2 tablespoons rice vinegar
2 teaspoons vegetable oil
100g (3½oz) firm tofu
1 teaspoon ground turmeric
a pinch of salt
2 spring onions, topped, tailed and chopped
2 slices of bread, toasted
2 sprigs of parsley or coriander, chopped

Place the avocado, tomato and rice vinegar in a bowl, toss to combine.

Place a frying pan over a medium heat, warm the oil and, using a wooden spoon, scramble the tofu with the ground turmeric and a pinch of salt, mixing well and cooking for a minute to get rid of the moisture. Add the spring onion and mix well.

Arrange the toast on each plate and spoon the avocado mix on top. Add the scrambled tofu mix and garnish with coriander or parsley.

egg + avocado smash on toast

serves 2

2 free-range eggs, boiled, poached or scrambled
2 slices of bread, toasted
½ red chilli, finely sliced
2 sprigs of coriander, leaves picked

for the tofu, edamame and avocado smash
40g (1½oz) cooked edamame beans
½ avocado
20g (¾oz) silken tofu
10ml (2 teaspoons) spicy vinegar (see page 178)
½ lime, juiced or 5ml (1 teaspoon) bottled lime juice
a pinch of salt

First make the tofu, edamame and avocado smash. Place all the ingredients in a food processor or blender and blitz to a chunky texture.

Now make the eggs of your choice – poached, boiled or scrambled.

Arrange a piece of toast on each plate and spread with the avocado smash. Top with the egg and garnish with chilli and coriander.

✴ Remove the eggs for a vegan dish.

✴ Use gluten-free bread for a gluten-free dish.

mackerel on toast

serves 2

100g (3½oz) smoked mackerel
2 free-range eggs
2 slices of bread, toasted
55ml (2fl oz) malt vinegar

10g (¼oz) butter
½ red chilli, sliced
2 sprigs of coriander or
  parsley, chopped

Using a fork, shred the smoked mackerel onto a plate.

Take deep pan, add water to cover ¾ of the pan and let it boil. In a separate bowl, crack the eggs carefully and add 30ml (1fl oz) of the malt vinegar. Once the water in the pan comes to a boil, add 20ml (⅔fl oz) of the malt vinegar, swirl the water and slowly add the eggs and bring water to boil. After a minute, turn the flame down and cook the eggs for a further 2 minutes. Slowly remove the poached eggs onto a plate.

Butter the toast, spoon the shredded mackerel on top and drizzle with the remaining vinegar.

Arrange the poached eggs on top, garnish with sliced chilli and chopped coriander or parsley.

● teriyaki mushrooms
● + avocado smash on toast

serves 2

1 tablespoon vegetable oil
200g (7oz) your favourite
  mushrooms, sliced
2 tablespoons Teriyaki Sauce
  (see page 177)

tofu, edamame + avocado
  smash (see page 40)
2 slices of bread, toasted

Warm the oil in a frying pan over a high heat and sauté the mushrooms until nearly cooked. Add the teriyaki sauce, turn down the heat and cook until sticky, then set aside.

Make the tofu, edamame and avocado smash. Arrange the toast on each plate and spread with the avocado smash. Top with the teriyaki mushrooms and enjoy.

....

✱ **Pushed for time? Why not use our own-brand teriyaki stir-fry sauce, instead of making it from scratch?**

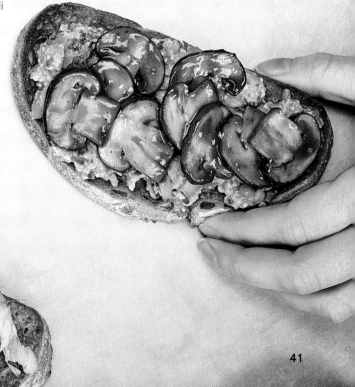

firecracker jackfruit hirata buns

You need to make the hirata buns, but it is well worth it.

serves 2

4 hirata buns (see page 180)
4 tablespoons firecracker sauce (see page 176)
1 carrot, grated or cut into julienne
¼ white radish (optional), grated or cut into julienne
¼ cucumber, grated or cut into julienne
½ red onion, finely sliced
150ml (5fl oz) rice vinegar
2 tablespoons vegetable oil
1 x 400g (14oz) tin jackfruit, well drained

Make sure your hirata buns are prepared as this can take up to 2 hours if you are making them from scratch. Prepare the firecracker sauce.

Put the carrot, white radish and cucumber into a large bowl, add the red onion, cover with the rice vinegar and leave for about 20 minutes.

Meanwhile steam your buns for 5–7 minutes.

Heat the oil in a wok or large pan, add the jackfruit and cook until hot and it starts to brown. When nearly ready, add the firecracker sauce and heat through for 30 seconds, turning the jackfruit in the sauce until coated.

Drain the slaw. Half-fill each bun with slaw, then add some firecracker jackfruit and drizzle with a little extra sauce.

✴ **If you're not a fan of jackfruit, try with your favourite mushroom.**

✴ **This dish is vegan if you are using plant-based milk in the hirata bun recipe.**

hoisin pulled duck hirata buns

Our take on the classic Chinese dish – duck wraps.

serves 2

1 duck leg

2 bay leaves

150ml (5fl oz) goose fat or olive oil

4 hirata buns (see page 180)

4 tablespoons spicy cherry hoisin sauce (see page 172)

salt and freshly ground black pepper

½ cucumber, grated or cut into julienne strips

Make sure your hirata buns are prepared as this can take up to 2 hours if you are making them from scratch. Preheat the oven to 150°C/300°F/gas mark 2.

Put the duck leg in a deep oven tin with the bay leaves, season with a pinch of salt and pepper, pour over the goose fat (or oil) and cover with foil. Cook in the oven for 2 hours.

Meanwhile, make your hoisin sauce.

Take the duck leg out of the goose fat (which you can use again). Using two forks, remove the meat from the bone and put in a bowl (making sure not to include any stray bits of bone), cover with the rich hoisin sauce and keep warm.

Steam the hirata buns for 5–7 minutes.

Half-fill each bun with cucumber, add the warm hoisin duck and maybe drizzle over a little more sauce.

✸ **To make this vegan, use grated seitan, but make sure you crisp it up.**

bacon roti wrap

sausage roti wrap

serves 2

1 tablespoon oil
4 back bacon rashers
2 free-range eggs
2 roti
2 tablespoons sriracha mayo
20g (¾oz) baby spinach, washed

Place a frying pan over a medium heat, warm the oil and cook the bacon rashers on both sides until they are nice and crisp. Transfer to a plate lined with kitchen paper to soak up any excess oil. Set aside and keep warm.

Crack an egg into a bowl and whisk well. Add the egg to an oiled frying pan and stir like you are making an omelette. Once the egg has just started to cook, place the roti on top so the two stick together.

Carefully flip the roti and egg over so that the roti warms in the pan, then transfer to a chopping board, egg-side up. Repeat with the other egg and roti.

Drizzle the sriracha mayo over each roti, then add the spinach and bacon rashers.

Roll the rotis nice and tight, then cut in half, serve and enjoy.

serves 2

2 Cumberland sausages
1 teaspoon oil
2 free-range eggs
2 roti
2 tablespoons sriracha mayo
20g (¾oz) baby spinach, washed

Preheat the oven to 180°C/350°F/gas mark 4.

Arrange the sausages on a foil-lined oven tray and cook in the oven for 12–15 minutes until well cooked. Remove from the oven, allow to cool a little, then slice each sausage lengthways into two long pieces.

Crack an egg into a bowl and whisk well. Add the egg to an oiled frying pan and stir like you are making an omelette. Once the egg has just started to cook, place the roti on top so the two stick together.

Carefully flip the roti and egg over so that the roti warms in the pan, then transfer to a chopping board, egg-side up. Repeat with the other egg and roti.

Drizzle the sriracha mayo over each roti, then add the spinach and sausage.

Roll the rotis nice and tight, then cut in half, serve and enjoy.

....

★ Replace the meat sausages with vegan sausages. We like to use vegan beetroot sausages!

chicken katsu sando

The ultimate katsu sandwich, with a spicy curry mayo.

serves 2

1 large chicken breast fillet
1 free-range egg, lightly beaten
25g (1oz) plain flour
50g (2oz) panko breadcrumbs
100ml (3½fl oz) vegetable oil, for frying
40g (1½oz) Savoy cabbage
40g (1½oz) kewpie mayonnaise
1 teaspoon curry paste
4 brioche slices, toasted
2 soft-boiled free-range eggs, sliced in half

Take a chicken breast and slice in half across the middle, like a burger bun.

Place the egg, flour and panko breadcrumbs in three separate wide, shallow bowls. First coat the chicken in flour, then dip into the egg and finally cover in breadcrumbs. Press the chicken into the breadcrumbs to ensure the meat is thoroughly coated and is nice and flat (the thinner the chicken breast, the quicker it will cook).

Place the oil in a saucepan over a medium heat and, when hot, shallow fry the breaded chicken for 3–4 minutes on each side. Transfer to a plate lined with kitchen paper to soak up the excess oil. If you haven't already, cook your eggs until soft boiled.

Bring a saucepan of water to the boil and blanch the Savoy cabbage for 30 seconds, then plunge into ice-cold water for a minute, drain and set aside. Mix the mayonnaise with the curry paste until smooth and well combined.

Spread two slices of toasted brioche with the curry mayo and arrange on each plate. Layer with the Savoy cabbage, fried chicken and sliced egg and finish with a slice of toast on top.

Slice your sandos in half with a sharp knife and enjoy!

✴ **The great thing about a sando is how you can switch it up to suit your dietary requirements and taste. To make this vegetarian, why not use panko-coated deep-fried aubergine instead of chicken?**

✴ **If you have some leftover katsu sauce, or have a jar of our wagamama katsu paste in your fridge, you could mix this with your mayo for the ultimate spread.**

shiok chicken bánh mi

Delicious, spicy baguettes Vietnamese-style.

serves 2

4 skinless chicken thighs

30g (1oz) shiok marinade (see page 173)

1 medium-size red onion, finely sliced

½ medium-size white radish, julienned

1 medium-size carrot, julienned

2 red radishes, topped, tailed and sliced into rounds

½ cucumber, julienned

90ml (3fl oz) pickling liquor (see page 178)

1 French baguette

2 tablespoons sriracha mayonnaise

2 sprigs of coriander, leaves picked

1 small red chilli, finely sliced

Preheat the oven to 180°C/200°C/400°F/gas mark 6.

Place the chicken thighs in a bowl with the shiok marinade and rub in well. Set aside to marinate for at least an hour.

Place the red onion, white radish and carrot in a container, add 60ml (2fl oz) of the pickling liquor and allow the veg to pickle for a minimum of 30 minutes. Use the remaining pickling liquor to pickle the red radish, again for a minimum of 30 minutes.

Once the mixed veg is pickled, drain off the excess pickling liquor, add the cucumber and toss to combine.

Arrange the marinated chicken on a tray and place in the oven for 20 minutes. Once cooked, allow to cool slightly and then slice.

Divide the baguette into portions and slice each in half. Spread with sriracha mayonnaise and fill with the Asian slaw and chicken. Place pickled red radish on top and garnish with coriander and chilli slices.

✸ To make this dish vegan, marinate chunky mushrooms instead of chicken and make sure your baguette is vegan.

✸ Grate your veg instead of julienning it to save time.

ssambap

korean bbq sirloin steak

serves 2

1 x 150–200g (6–7oz) beef sirloin steak, finely sliced

1 tablespoon vegetable oil

2 tablespoons Korean bbq sauce (see page 172)

1 gem lettuce, leaves divided and washed

¼ cucumber, julienned

2 spring onions, topped, tailed and sliced at an angle

1 small red chilli, finely sliced

1 teaspoon chilli oil (optional)

salt and freshly ground black pepper

Season the sirloin and drizzle with 5ml (1 teaspoon) of oil.

Heat the remaining oil in a medium-size pan over a high heat and stir-fry the steak for a minute. Add the Korean bbq sauce and toss for 1 minute, then take off the heat.

Take six large lettuce leaves and fill with the steak, cucumber, spring onion and red chilli. For an added kick of spice, drizzle each lettuce leaf with a dash of chilli oil, if using.

spicy teriyaki chicken

serves 2

1 teaspoon ginger paste

1 teaspoon garlic paste

4 sprigs of coriander, finely chopped

2 red chillies, finely sliced

2 medium-size chicken breasts, cut into 3mm (⅛in) slices

1 tablespoon oil

2 tablespoons spicy teriyaki sauce (see page 177)

1 gem lettuce, leaves divided and washed

¼ cucumber, julienned

4 spring onions, topped, tailed and sliced at an angle

1 teaspoon chilli oil (optional)

salt and freshly ground black pepper

Place the ginger paste, garlic paste, chopped coriander, 1 chopped chilli, salt and pepper into a bowl and mix. Add the chopped chicken to the mix and marinate for 30 minutes. Cover the chicken in the marinade, season with salt and pepper and set aside to marinate for 30 minutes.

Heat the oil in a medium-size pan over a high heat and stir-fry the marinated chicken until cooked. Add the spicy teriyaki sauce and toss for 1 minute, then take off the heat.

Take six large lettuce leaves and fill with chicken, cucumber, spring onion and red chilli. For an added kick of spice, drizzle each lettuce leaf with a dash of chilli oil, if using.

✶ **Use tamari sauce to make this gluten-free.**

cherry hoisin roast duck

serves 2

1 teaspoon ginger paste

1 teaspoon garlic paste

1 teaspoon Chinese five spice powder

1 lemongrass stalk, tough outer leaves
   removed, crushed with the side of a
   knife and finely sliced

1 red chilli, finely sliced

4 sprigs of coriander, finely chopped

2 medium-size duck legs

1 tablespoon vegetable oil

2 tablespoons spicy cherry hoisin sauce
   (see page 172)

1 gem lettuce, leaves divided and washed

¼ cucumber, julienned

2 spring onions, sliced at an angle

1 teaspoon chilli oil (optional)

salt and freshly ground black pepper

Preheat the oven to 190°C/375°F/gas mark 5.

Place the ginger and garlic pastes in a bowl and mix to combine with the Chinese five spice powder, lemongrass, most of the chilli and the coriander. Cover the duck legs in the marinade, season with salt and pepper and set aside to marinate for an hour.

Arrange the duck legs on a lightly oiled baking tray and place in the oven for 45 minutes. Allow to cool, then shred the duck meat off the bone. Check over and remove any small bones or cartilage. Add your spicy cherry hoisin sauce and mix into the warm duck meat.

Take six large lettuce leaves and fill with shredded duck, cucumber, spring onion and red chilli. For an added kick of spice, drizzle each lettuce leaf with a dash of chilli oil, if using.

....

★ For a vegan option for these dishes, switch out the meat for jackfruit: Drain a tin of jackfruit in brine, pat it dry until all excess moisture is gone, then shallow-fry the jackfruit in pan of oil for a few minutes on each side. Allow to cool, then toss in the sauces used in each recipe.

★ Use tamari sauce to make this gluten-free.

2.

bowls of goodness

A whole lot of goodness goes into a wagamama bowl. The freshest of veg, the most balanced of broths, just the right amount of noodles or rice, and the fiercest Asian flavours. Together, these ingredients make up the soulful wagamama bowlfuls you know and love.

In this chapter, you'll learn how to add serious soul to your bowls – the wagamama way. Want a taste of what's to come?

Think bright noodle salads, steaming gyoza ramen, aromatic fish curry and chicken marinated in the flavours of Malaysia. Beyond this page, there's a bowl for everyone.

hiyashi proteins

salmon

serves 1

1 teaspoon vegetable oil
1 fillet salmon (120–150g/4–5oz)
a pinch of salt and pepper

Heat the oil in a medium-size pan and cook the salmon fillet, seasoned with a pinch of salt and pepper, over a medium heat for 3–4 minutes on each side or until fully cooked through.

Take the pan off the heat and shred the salmon using a fork.

sriracha prawns

serves 1

5 king prawns
1 tablespoon sriracha sauce
1 teaspoon vegetable oil

Marinate the prawns in the sriracha sauce for at least 30 minutes.

Heat the oil in a medium-size pan or wok, add the prawns and cook over a low flame for a minute, then turn over and cook for another minute. Take off the heat.

miso veg

serves 1

30g (1oz) longstem broccoli
1 tablespoon vegetable oil
20g (¾oz) curly kale, roughly chopped
75g (3oz) mixed mushrooms, sliced
1 tablespoon miso sesame dressing (see page 173)

Blanch the longstem broccoli in boiling water for 2 minutes, then plunge into ice-cold water, drain and set aside.

Heat the oil in a medium-size pan or wok, add the kale, broccoli and mushrooms and toss over a high heat for a minute. Add the miso sesame dressing, toss and cook for a further minute.

spicy teriyaki duck

serves 1

1 duck leg
a pinch of salt and pepper
2 teaspoons ginger paste
2 teaspoons garlic paste
1 teaspoon vegetable oil
2 tablespoons spicy teriyaki sauce (see page 177)

Season the duck leg with salt and pepper and rub all over with the ginger and garlic paste. Set aside to marinate for an hour.

Preheat the oven to 190°C/375°F/gas mark 5. Place the duck leg on a lightly oiled baking tray and cook for 45 minutes, then allow to cool and shred onto a plate. Check over for any small bones or cartilage, and add the duck meat to a bowl. Add the spicy teriyaki sauce to the duck meat and mix well.

teriyaki chicken

serves 1

2 skinless boneless chicken thighs, sliced into strips
a pinch of salt and pepper
½ teaspoon ginger paste
½ teaspoon garlic paste
1 teaspoon vegetable oil
1 tablespoon teriyaki sauce (see page 177)
   or use 1 tablespoon of our retail product

Season the chicken thigh pieces with salt and pepper and rub all over with the ginger and garlic pastes. Set aside to marinate for at least 30 minutes.

Heat the oil in a medium size pan, add the chicken slices and cook for about 5–10 minutes until fully cooked. Then add the teriyaki sauce and stir for a few minutes until the chicken is well coated.

hiyashi salad components

turmeric cauliflower

serves 1

50g (2oz) cauliflower, cut into small florets
1½ teaspoons ground turmeric
1 tablespoon vegetable oil

Place the cauliflower in a bowl and toss with the turmeric and 10ml (2 teaspoons) oil until well coated.

Preheat the oven to 160°C/325°F/gas mark 3. Drizzle the remaining oil over a baking tray and arrange the cauliflower on top. Cook in the oven for 10 minutes. Use hot or allow to cool for later use.

tofu + edamame guac

serves 1

40g (1½oz) cooked edamame beans
½ ripe avocado, prepped
20g (¾oz) silken tofu
10ml (2 teaspoons) spicy vinegar (see page 178)
½ lime, juiced (or 5ml/1 teaspoon bottled)
a pinch of salt
a pinch of toasted sesame seeds, to garnish

Place all the ingredients except the sesame seeds in a container and, using a stick blender, blitz to a coarse texture. Once plated up, garnish with sesame seeds.

white dressing

makes about 150ml (5fl oz)

100g (3½oz) vegan mayonnaise
20g Dijon mustard
¼ block silken tofu (75g)
1 tablespoon miso paste
1 tablespoon spicy vinegar (see page 178)
5g tamari soy sauce
1 lime, juiced
45ml water
10g caster sugar

Measure all the ingredients into a container and, using a stick blender, blend until smooth.

Decant into a dry, airtight container and store in the refrigerator – this recipe will make a batch of dressing and you only need 30ml (1fl oz) for one salad so you can use it throughout the week. It will keep for about 3 days.

pickled Asian slaw

serves 1

¼ carrot, julienned
¼ red onion, julienned
¼ white radish, julienned
50ml (2fl oz) rice vinegar
¼ cucumber, julienned

Place the carrot, red onion and radish in a bowl and cover with rice vinegar. Set aside for 30 minutes, maximum.

Once pickled, drain the vinegar from the veg and now stir through the cucumber – this is your pickled Asian slaw.

glass noodles

100g (3½oz) glass bean noodles
1 teaspoon spicy vinegar (see page 178)
1 red chilli, finely sliced

Cook the noodles, following the packet instructions, then drain. Once plated up, drizzle over the spicy vinegar and garnish with chilli.

sliced radish

20g (¾oz) baby red radish, finely sliced

chicken harusame salad

Harusame means 'spring rain' in Japanese, which is represented in this dish by the glass bean noodles. This dish is a great light lunch option.

serves 2

2 medium chicken breasts
1 teaspoon ginger paste
1 teaspoon garlic paste
a large pinch of salt
a pinch of pepper
1 lemongrass stalk
4 sprigs of coriander
1 red chilli, sliced
80g (3oz) glass bean noodles
2 teaspoons tamari soy sauce
60g (2½oz) edamame beans
small bunch of mint, leaves picked and
    finely sliced
30ml (1fl oz) spicy vinegar (see
    page 178)
60g (2½oz) adzuki beans from a tin,
    drained and rinsed
40g (1½oz) pea shoots
60g (2½oz) Asian slaw (see page 64)
50g (2oz) red radishes, sliced into thin
    roundels
1 teaspoon toasted coconut chips
1 teaspoon fried shallots

Mix the chicken breasts in a bowl with the ginger paste, garlic paste, salt and pepper and leave to marinate for at least 30 minutes in the fridge.

Fill a deep pan (with a lid) with 500ml (18fl oz) water. Using the back of a knife, smash the lemongrass and add to the water along with the coriander sprigs and red chilli. Add the marinated chicken breasts, cover the pan and bring to the boil. Cook for about 12 minutes, until the chicken is cooked through and there is no pink meat.

Lift the chicken out of the broth and allow to cool before shredding into thin pieces.

Cook the glass bean noodles as per the packet instructions. Once cooked, stir a couple of times, drain off the water, and then toss the noodles in the tamari sauce.

Blanch the edamame beans in boiling water for 1 minute, then plunge into ice-cold water and leave for a further 2 minutes. Drain and set aside.

Mix half of the mint into the spicy vinegar and reserve the rest for the garnish.

In a mixing bowl, add the adzuki beans, edamame beans, glass noodles, pea shoots, Asian slaw, red radishes and finally the shredded chicken. Toss well, ensuring all the ingredients are well combined.

Add the spicy vinegar and toss well. Divide between two bowls, and garnish each with coconut chips, fried shallots and the remaining finely sliced mint.

✱ **This salad also works well with salmon or with tofu to make it a vegan dish.**

coconut seafood broth

A nourishing broth with succulent seafood and tender vegetables.

serves 2

50g (2oz) longstem broccoli, trimmed

2 medium-size pak choi, destalked and leaves separated

125g (4½oz) rice noodle sticks

2 tablespoons oil

1 x 120–140g (4–5oz) salmon fillet, sliced into 8–10 chunks

8 raw king prawns

1 small squid tube, sliced into rings

8 mussels, deshelled

8 queen scallops

90ml (3fl oz) coconut milk

1 tablespoon fish sauce

a few sprigs of coriander, leaves picked

1 red chilli, thinly sliced

for the broth

400ml (14fl oz) vegetable stock

3 tablespoons coriander seeds

3 tablespoons cumin seeds

5 sprigs of mint

5 sprigs of coriander

1 tablespoon tamarind paste

2 lemongrass stalks

First make the broth. Place all the ingredients except for the lemongrass in a saucepan and bring to the boil over a medium heat. Using the back of a knife, crush the lemongrass and add it to the stock. Cook for 10 minutes, then take off the heat, strain the broth into a container and set aside.

Next, prepare the vegetables. Blanch the longstem broccoli in boiling water for 2 minutes, then plunge into ice-cold water, drain and set aside. Slice any big pak choi leaves into two and also set aside.

Place the rice noodles in a saucepan and cover with boiling water. Leave for 5 minutes, or until the noodles are cooked, then drain and divide between two serving bowls.

Place a deep pan on the hob over a medium heat, add the oil and, once hot, stir-fry the salmon chunks and seafood for 2–3 minutes.

Add the vegetables and broth to the pan and bring to the boil. Add the coconut milk and fish sauce and stir well. Once fragrant, remove from the heat and ladle into the bowls, over the noodles, and garnish with coriander leaves and sliced red chilli.

✶ **If you are vegetarian or don't fancy seafood but like the sound of this delicious coconut broth, you could pack the dish with more of your favourite veg and leave out the fish sauce.**

mandarin
chicken salad

Fresh and citrussy, with a delicious Asian twist. You will only need 90ml (3½fl oz) of the dressing for two salad portions.

serves 2

1 small tin mandarin segments
1 lemongrass stalk
5 sprigs of coriander, 1 sprig of leaves
    picked
1 red chilli
1 teaspoon oil
1 medium-size red onion, thinly sliced
50g (2oz) mangetout
4 spring onions, topped, tailed and finely
    sliced at an angle
100g (3½oz) mixed salad leaves
60g (2oz) roasted cashew nuts
2 teaspoons toasted sesame seeds

for the marinade
½ teaspoon ginger paste
½ teaspoon garlic paste
a pinch of salt and a pinch of cracked
    black pepper
2 medium-size chicken breasts

for the dressing (makes 450ml/ 15fl oz)
100ml (3½fl oz) mandarin juice
1 tablespoon sugar
1 tablespoon cracked black pepper
1 heaped tablespoon English mustard
40ml (1½fl oz) rice vinegar
200ml (7fl oz) vegetable oil
50ml (2fl oz) sesame oil
50ml (2 fl oz) soy sauce

First make the marinade: mix the ginger and garlic paste with salt and pepper in a bowl. Add the chicken breast and coat thoroughly, then set aside to marinate for a minimum of 30 minutes.

Open the mandarin tin and drain the liquid; reserving the juices for the dressing and keeping the segments for the salad.

Place all the dressing ingredients in a mixing bowl and whisk until the sugar is dissolved and you have a smooth dressing.

Take a deep pan (with a lid) and fill with 500ml (18fl oz) water. Using the back of a knife, smash the lemongrass and add to the water along with 4 sprigs of coriander and the red chilli. Add the marinated chicken breasts, cover the pan and bring to the boil. Cook for about 12 minutes, until the chicken is cooked through (no pink meat).

Once cooked, lift the chicken breast out of the broth and allow to cool before shredding into thin pieces.

Lightly oil a frying pan and cook the red onion over a medium heat until lightly caramelised, then set aside.

Blanch the mangetout in boiling water for 2 minutes, then plunge into ice-cold water, drain and slice in half lengthways before setting aside.

Now we are ready to assemble the salad: take a big mixing bowl and add the shredded chicken, mandarin segments, blanched mangetout, caramelised red onion, spring onion and roasted cashew nuts and mix well. Add the mixed salad leaves and 90ml (3fl oz) of the dressing and toss together gently.

Divide the salad between two plates and garnish with coriander leaves and toasted sesame seeds.

✦ **Replace the chicken with tofu to make this dish vegan.**

✦ **Keep the leftover salad dressing in a dry airtight container or jar and refrigerate so you can use it again.**

tempura

A typical Japanese dish, where the light crispy batter gives a delicious savoury crunch to meat, fish or vegetables.

serves 2

prawn

10 raw king prawns, deshelled with tail on

steak

120g (4oz) sirloin steak, cut into 5mm (¼in) slices and seasoned with a pinch each of salt and black pepper

mushroom (vegan)

1 king oyster mushroom, cut into 6 wedges

for the tempura

100g (3½oz) tempura flour
120ml (4fl oz) chilled sparkling water
250ml (8fl oz) vegetable oil, for deep frying

for the garnish

a few sprigs of coriander, leaves picked
1 red chilli, sliced
1 lime, cut into wedges
30g (1oz) sriracha mayonnaise

Place the tempura flour in a mixing bowl and slowly whisk in the chilled sparkling water until smooth. Do not worry if there are any small lumps.

Add the oil to a large saucepan over a medium-high heat for a few minutes until hot. To check if the oil is ready, add a drop of the tempura batter – it is ready if the batter sizzles and doesn't drop to the bottom of the pan.

Using a chopstick, dip each of the prawns, mushroom or steak pieces into the batter until thoroughly coated. Carefully lower the battered pieces into the oil, making sure the hot oil does not splash. Work in batches to ensure you don't overcrowd the pan.

If making the mushroom tempura, fry for 2–3 minutes or until golden. If cooking the prawn or beef, fry for about 4–5 minutes or until golden to ensure you cook the inside. Then remove with a slotted spoon and transfer to a plate lined with kitchen paper to soak up any excess oil.

Place the tempura on a serving plate and garnish with the coriander, sliced chillies and lime wedges. Serve with the sriracha mayonnaise on the side.

miso ramen

A warming noodle broth with both heat and crunch.

serves 2

800ml (28fl oz) chicken stock

1 tablespoon miso paste

1 ½ teaspoons shichimi powder

2 teaspoons chilli oil

2 nests ramen noodles

2 chicken breasts, sliced into thin strips

2 small garlic cloves, finely chopped

¼ leek, sliced lengthways and coarsely chopped

½ carrot, grated

40g (1 ½oz) mangetout, trimmed

150g (5oz) beansprouts

1 tablespoon soy sauce or tamari

2 spring onions, topped, tailed and sliced at an angle

a sprinkle of sesame seeds

a few drops of chilli oil

Place the stock in a deep pan and bring to a gentle simmer. Mix the miso paste with the shichimi powder and chilli oil until you have a smooth paste and then add this to the stock, whisking to ensure there are no lumps.

Cook two portions of ramen noodles, following the packet instructions, and once cooked, drain and divide between two ramen bowls.

Place a wok or large pan over a high heat, warm the oil, add the chicken and cook for a minute. Add the garlic and vegetables and stir-fry, tossing occasionally to ensure you caramelise the vegetables.

Add the soy sauce, stir and then remove from the heat (checking to ensure the chicken is cooked through).

Ladle the hot chicken miso stock over the noodles in each bowl, using chopsticks to separate the noodles and make a base. Add the stir-fried chicken and vegetables in a pile on top and garnish with spring onion, sesame seeds and chilli oil.

✶ This dish is all about the delicate broth, so switch out the chicken stock for vegetable stock, and the chicken for tofu, mushrooms or a meat substitute to make it vegan (and make sure you're using vegan noodles). This dish is gluten-free if you use the tamari instead of soy sauce.

tofu turmeric salad

Beautifully marinated tofu makes this salad fun and full of flavour.

serves 2

200g (7oz) firm tofu, cut into 2.5cm
   cubes

30g (1oz) shiok marinade (see page 173)

3 tablespoons vegetable oil

½ sweet potato, peeled, washed and cut
   into 2.5cm (1in) chunks

a small pinch of salt

a small pinch of pepper

50g (2oz) red radishes, sliced into thin
   roundels

20ml (⅔fl oz) pickling liquor (see
   page 178)

50g (2oz) edamame beans

50g (2oz) cherry tomatoes, sliced in half

150g (5oz) mixed salad leaves

30ml (1fl oz) wagamama salad dressing
   (see page 178)

to garnish

small bunch of coriander, leaves picked

6 red chillies, sliced

1 teaspoon toasted coconut chips

4 mint leaves, finely sliced

Preheat the oven to 170°C/325°F/gas mark 3.

Place the tofu in a container and mix with the shiok marinade. Pour 1 tablespoon of the oil into a medium pan over a medium heat, and, when hot, add the tofu and cook until all sides are lightly browned. Remove the tofu chunks from the pan.

Arrange the sweet potato chunks on a tray oiled with the remaining 2 tablespoons of oil. Season with the salt and pepper. Cook the sweet potatoes in the preheated oven for 10 minutes, then remove the tray and allow the to cool slightly. Decant the sweet potatoes into a container.

Place the radishes in a bowl with the pickling liquor. Leave for 10 minutes, then drain off the liquor and set the radishes aside.

Blanch the edamame beans in boiling water for 1 minute, then plunge into ice-cold water and leave for a further 2 minutes. Drain and set aside.

Take a large mixing bowl, and add the warm tofu pieces, warm sweet potatoes, edamame beans, pickled red radishes and cherry tomatoes. Mix well. Add the salad leaves and the salad dressing, and mix gently.

Divide the salad between two bowls, making sure there are equal quantities of all ingredients.

Garnish with the coriander, chillies, coconut chips and mint.

korean fish curry

A fragrant red curry, inspired by the flavours of Seoul.

serves 2

250ml (8fl oz) Korean red curry sauce
    (see page 169)
100g (3½ oz) jasmine rice
4 longstem broccoli
1 pak choi, destalked and leaves
    separated
6 mangetout, trimmed
1 tablespoon vegetable oil
1 salmon fillet (120–150g/4–5oz), sliced
    into small chunks
8 queen scallops
4 king prawns
a few sprigs of coriander, leaves picked
½ red chilli, thinly sliced
½ lime, cut into wedges

Follow the recipe on page 169 to make your Korean red curry sauce and have it on a simmer while you prepare the rest of the dish.

Cook 100g (3½oz) jasmine rice as per instructions on the packet (this should make around double the amount of cooked rice). Then divide between two serving bowls and set aside.

Next, prepare the vegetables. Blanch the longstem broccoli in boiling water for 2 minutes, then plunge into ice-cold water, drain and set aside. Slice any large pak choi leaves into two and also set aside along with the mangetout.

Place a wok or large pan on a high heat, add the oil and, once hot, stir-fry the salmon and seafood for 2–3 minutes. Add the vegetables and red curry sauce and stir to combine. Reduce the heat and simmer for about 10 minutes until the seafood is fully cooked.

Remove from the heat and ladle into the serving bowls, over the rice, and garnish with coriander, sliced chilli and a lime wedge.

✱ **If you love the sound of this curry sauce but don't eat seafood, you could use your favourite alternative protein instead (we think smoked tempeh works great) to make the dish vegan.**

shu's shiok chicken

This dish was created by our executive chef Surendra Yeiju in collaboration with Shu Han Lee, a fantastic London-based Singaporean chef and author.

serves 2

50g (2oz) shiok marinade (see page 173)

4 medium chicken thighs

60g (2oz) red radishes, sliced

30ml (1fl oz) pickling liquor (see page 178)

5 mint leaves, finely sliced

30ml (1fl oz) spicy vinegar (see page 178)

1 lime, halved

1 teaspoon caster sugar

120ml (4fl oz) raisukaree sauce (see page 178)

200g (7oz) sticky rice, cooked (see page 178)

80g (3oz) pickled Asian slaw (see page 64)

small bunch of coriander, leaves picked

1 red chilli, finely sliced

1 teaspoon toasted coconut chips

Preheat the oven to 170°C/325°F/gas mark 3.

Rub the shiok marinade into the chicken thighs and set aside for 30 minutes. Place the marinated chicken on an oiled tray, and cook in the oven for 20 minutes.

Add the radishes to a bowl with the pickling liquor and set aside for 30 minutes. Once pickled, drain the liquid away.

Cook your rice, and while it is cooking, continue with preparing the other ingredients. In a bowl, mix the finely sliced mint with the spicy vinegar.

Roll the lime pieces in the sugar. Place a small pan over a medium heat, and, when hot, add the lime pieces and caramelise for one minute. Set aside.

In another pan, gently reheat the raisukaree sauce.

Divide the cooked rice between two serving bowls. Remove the chicken thighs from the oven, cut into 2cm (1¾in) slices and divide the slices between the bowls. Drizzle the raisukaree sauce over the chicken.

Arrange the pickled red radish, Asian slaw, coriander, sliced chillies and caramelised lime in the bowls. Sprinkle over the coconut chips and serve.

✶ **To make this dish vegan, use portobello mushrooms marinated in shiok marinade.**

✶ **You could also use our Thai-style raisukaree paste to make the raisukaree sauce.**

steamed yasai gyoza

Beautiful Japanese dumplings filled with vegan goodness, great to accompany a meal or enjoy as a snack.

serves 2

150g (5oz) firm tofu, cubed
50g (2oz) edamame beans
30g (1oz) water chestnuts, finely chopped
30g (1oz) red adzuki beans, rinsed and
    drained well
2 spring onions, finely chopped
1 teaspoon ground turmeric
1½ teaspoons soy sauce
1 tablespoon amai sauce
1 tablespoon vegetable oil
a pinch of salt
10 gyoza skins (see page 181)

Place the tofu in a mixing bowl.

Blanch the edamame beans by plunging them into boiling water for 2–3 minutes, drain, mash slightly, then add to the mixing bowl.

Add the water chestnuts, red adzuki beans, spring onions, turmeric, soy sauce, amai sauce and a pinch of salt and mix well.

Place the gyoza skins in a pile on a chopping board, keeping them covered until you use them. Have ready a small bowl of water to seal the gyozas.

Take a gyoza skin, place a teaspoon of mixture in the centre, rub water around the edge and seal tightly, crimping the edges in whatever way you like. Repeat for the remaining skins. Once all gyozas are filled, place in the fridge to set.

To make steamed gyoza (like in this photo), add your gyozas to a lightly oiled pan with a matching lid on a low–medium heat and add a few tablespoons of water. Place the lid on top and steam for around 5–6 minutes until the skins become transparent. Once all the water has evaporated, add a drizzle of oil over the gyoza and allow to brown on the bottom.

✱ **If you want crunchy gyoza, why not deep-fry them instead? Place them into a saucepan of hot oil until golden brown.**

yasai gyoza ramen

You can use whichever gyoza you like to make this delicious ramen your own.

serves 2

10 steamed yasai gyoza (see page 86)

1 pak choi/bok choi

2 tablespoons vegetable oil

1 teaspoon shichimi

2 nests vegan noodles

600ml (20fl oz) vegetable stock

2 tablespoons veg stir-fry sauce (we like Lee Kum Kee sauce)

2 tablespoons vegan chilli sambal paste (see page 172)

2 spring onions, julienned

5g (1 teaspoon) fresh coriander

1 teaspoon chilli oil

If you've made your gyoza especially for this dish, keep them warm whilst preparing the rest of the ingredients. If you have some uncooked yasai gyoza left over from a previous recipe, fry or steam them (whichever you prefer) according to the instructions on page 86.

Cut the pak choi in half lengthways so you have two pieces and wash well to remove any grit from in between the leaves. Leave to drain.

Heat a dash of oil in a pan, add the pak choi halves and leave for a minute. Turn over and cook on the other side. The pak choi should look slightly charred. Once cooked sprinkle with shichimi, set aside and keep warm.

Cook the noodles according to the instructions on the packet.

Stir the veg stir-fry sauce into the vegetable stock until well combined.

Place the cooked noodles in two hot bowls and pour over the stock mixture.

Arrange the yasai gyoza and roasted pak choi on top of the noodles and add the vegan chilli sambal paste.

Garnish with spring onions, coriander and a dash of chilli oil.

✦ **If you want your gyoza to have an extra crunch, you could deep-fry instead of steaming them.**

moyashi soba

One of our original wagamama restaurant dishes, updated for today.

serves 2

45g sun-dried tomatoes
½ tablespoon miso paste
1 teaspoon chilli paste
800ml (28fl oz) vegetable stock
4 longstem broccoli, trimmed
2 nests ramen noodles
1 tablespoon vegetable oil
½ courgette, sliced lengthways and into
    large chunks
50g (2oz) mangetout, trimmed
¼ leek, sliced lengthways and into
    large chunks
4 asparagus, sliced at an angle
150g (5oz) beansprouts
3 tablespoons soy sauce
2 spring onions, topped, tailed and sliced
    at an angle
1 tablespoon sesame seeds

Place the sun-dried tomatoes, miso paste, chilli paste and 30ml (1fl oz) of the vegetable stock in a deep bowl and, using a stick blender, make a smooth paste.

Blanch the longstem broccoli in boiling water for 2 minutes, then plunge into ice-cold water, drain and set aside.

Cook two portions of ramen noodles, following the instructions on the packaging and, once cooked, drain and divide between two ramen bowls.

Place a wok or large pan over a high heat, warm the oil and stir-fry the courgette, mangetout, leek, longstem broccoli, asparagus and beansprouts, tossing occasionally and ensuring the veg is caramelised but still firm. Add the soy sauce and give a final toss.

In a separate saucepan, place the remaining vegetable stock and bring it to a gentle simmer. Add the paste, whisking to ensure there are no lumps.

Ladle the hot stock over the noodles in each bowl, using chopsticks to separate the noodles and make a base. Add the stir-fried vegetables in a pile on top and garnish with spring onion and sesame seeds.

✳ **Use rice stick noodles and tamari sauce instead of soy sauce to make the dish non-gluten and vegan.**

3.

ways
with
the wok

There's no one way to work a wok. In fact, there are hundreds. A staple of any Japanese kitchen, the wok is responsible for some of wagamama's most beloved dishes. Fire up fresh new favourites or recreate a wagamama classic. This chapter will have you tossing, tasting, saucing and stirring, all at the same time.

Give new life to rice with our nasi goreng recipe, create corn on the cob sticky ribs, or simply toss fresh flavours together with your favourite noodles. The world is your wok.

Don't have a wok? Don't worry – all the dishes in this chapter can also be cooked in a large frying pan.

corn ribs

Corn on (or off) the cob
never tasted so good.

serves 2

2 corn on the cob
3 tablespoons sticky vegan sauce (see
    page 169)
1 tablespoon white miso paste
1 tablespoon vegetable oil
a few sprigs of coriander, leaves picked
    and chopped
1 small red chilli, finely sliced

Bring a pan of water to the boil, add the corn on the cob and cook for
7–9 minutes to soften slightly. Using a slotted spoon, lift out of the water,
drain and allow to cool.

Using a sharp knife, carefully slice the corn off the cob into rib-like strips, or
rounds if easier.

Place the sticky vegan sauce and miso paste in a bowl and whisk to a smooth
paste.

Place a wok or large pan over a medium heat, warm the oil, then add the corn
ribs and stir-fry, tossing regularly to get an even caramelisation all over.

Turn down the heat, pour over the sauce and mix and toss until the corn is
thoroughly coated.

Serve garnished with coriander and sliced chilli.

✱ **Cut the corn into roundels instead if you're struggling to recreate the
rib shape.**

chilli beef udon

A warming plate of spicy teriyaki noodles – a great dish for steak lovers.

serves 2

1 x 250–300g (9–10oz) sirloin steak, cut into 5mm (¼in) slices

2 tablespoons oil

1 medium-size pak choi, leaves separated

½ red onion, thinly sliced

½ leek, chopped in half lengthways and finely sliced at an angle

4 asparagus stems, each chopped into 3

100g (3½oz) beansprouts

1 free-range egg, beaten

250g (9oz) cooked udon noodles

30ml (1fl oz) spicy teriyaki sauce (see page 177)

a few sprigs of coriander, leaves picked and chopped

1 red chilli, sliced

salt and cracked black pepper

Season the steak with salt and pepper.

Place a medium-size frying pan over a high heat, add the oil and, when hot, stir-fry the steak to sear the edges. Add all of the vegetables and toss in the pan.

Turn the heat down to medium, add the beaten egg and udon noodles and cook, stirring all the time, so that the egg scrambles throughout the dish.

Add the spicy teriyaki sauce and mix well until all the stir-fry is coated in the sauce.

Divide between two plates and garnish with coriander and sliced chilli.

✸ **To make this dish vegetarian, use a mixture of shiitake and oyster mushrooms, instead of the steak.**

kaisen gohan

An 'at home' take on a dish we used to serve in our restaurants, this is great for seafood lovers.

serves 2

4 longstem broccoli
½ pak choi, leaves separated
1 tablespoon vegetable oil
1cm (½in) piece of ginger, finely chopped
1 garlic clove, finely chopped
8 raw king prawns
6 queen scallops
6 mussels
6 squid rings
75ml (3fl oz) soy sauce
75ml (3fl oz) water
1 teaspoon fish sauce
pinch of salt
½ teaspoon sugar
1½ teaspoons potato starch
250g (9oz) cooked udon noodles
1 small red chilli, finely sliced
a pinch of shichimi powder

Blanch the longstem broccoli in boiling water for 2 minutes, then plunge into ice-cold water and drain. Slice any big pak choi leaves into two and also set aside.

Place a wok or large pan over a high heat, warm the oil, then add the ginger and garlic and stir-fry for 30 seconds. Add all the seafood and vegetables and stir-fry, tossing continuously.

When nearly cooked, add the soy sauce, water and fish sauce and bring to the boil. Season with salt and sugar to taste.

In a small bowl, add a dash of water to the potato starch and mix into a to a thick paste, then stir this through the stir-fry to thicken the mixture. Once thick enough to coat the noodles, turn the heat down and gently simmer to keep hot.

Bring a pan of water to the boil, add the udon noodles for 30 seconds, then drain.

Divide the noodles between two plates, spoon the seafood and veg mix on top and drizzle over the sauce. Garnish with chilli and shichimi powder and serve.

✦ **If you want to cheat with the seafood, why not buy a seafood mix?**

kakushin udon

A spicy vegan noodle dish, inspired by Japan and reimagined here by our wagamama chefs.

serves 1

2 tablespoons amai sauce (see page 176)

2 tablespoons firecracker sauce (see page 176)

250g (9oz) cooked udon noodles

1 tablespoon vegetable oil

1 small red onion, thinly sliced

4 shiitake mushrooms, thinly sliced

6 mangetout, sliced lengthways into thin strips

1 small carrot, grated

1 garlic clove, finely chopped

¼ sweet potato, grated

100g (3½oz) beansprouts

½ teaspoon shichimi powder

1 tablespoon pickled ginger

In a small bowl, mix the amai and firecracker sauces together until well combined.

Place a wok or large pan over a high heat, warm the oil, then add all the vegetables and stir-fry for a minute, tossing and mixing well. Add the noodles and toss again.

Turn down the heat, add the sauce, mix and stir-fry well.

Take the pan off the heat and divide the stir-fry between two plates. Garnish with shichimi powder and pickled ginger.

✱ **Why not save time and use our off-the-shelf firecracker and pad Thai sauces, instead of making your own?**

amai udon

A comforting bowl of stir-fried noodles packed with tofu, prawns and veg.

serves 2

300–500g (10oz–1lb 2oz) cooked udon
    noodles (depending on how carb-heavy
    you want your meal to be)
1 leek, trimmed
1 free-range egg
1 tablespoon vegetable oil
100g (3½oz) firm tofu, cut into 2.5cm
    (1in) cubes
10 large cooked prawns
1 medium red onion, sliced
200g (7oz) beansprouts, rinsed
30ml (1fl oz) amai sauce (see page 176)
1 tablespoon ground peanuts
½ lime, cut into wedges

Cut the leek in half lengthways and then into 5mm (¼in) thick slices, then wash well and drain. Crack an egg into a bowl and gently whisk.

Place the oil in a medium pan over a medium heat, and, when hot, add the tofu and cook until all sides are lightly browned.

Add the prawns, leeks, red onions and beansprouts and stir-fry on high heat. Add the whisked egg and lightly scramble the egg through the vegetables.

Add the udon noodles, reduce the heat and stir-fry for 1–2 minutes.

Now add the amai sauce, mix and toss well. The sauce should coat the dish well and the noodles should have a good glaze on them. Take off the flame and pile onto a serving plate.

Sprinkle over the ground peanuts and garnish with lime wedges.

✱ **Remove the prawns and add more tofu if you want a vegetarian dish.**

✱ **To make this gluten-free, use rice noodles.**

✱ **Instead of Amai sauce you could use our pad Thai sauce, which is tamarind-based.**

sticky mushrooms and butternut squash stir-fry

A quick and easy vegan stir-fry with the special wagamama smokey barbeque sauce, varbeque.

serves 2

1 butternut squash, bulb-end
4 king oyster mushrooms
1 tablespoon oil
60ml (2fl oz) varbeque sauce (see page 169)
1 small red chilli
1 teaspoon toasted sesame seeds

Preheat the oven to 170°C/325°F/gas mark 3.

Cut off the bulb end of the butternut squash and peel it using a peeler. Cut in half and scoop out the seeds with a spoon, cut each half into two, then cut into 5mm (¼in) slices.

Cut the king oysters into half and then half again, so each mushroom is in 8 equal pieces.

Place the butternut squash into a roasting tray and drizzle with 5ml (1 teaspoon) oil. Roast for 12 minutes until crisp, take out and cool down

Place wok or wide-based pan on a medium heat, add the rest of the oil and once hot add the king oysters and stir-fry the mushrooms until they caramelise.

Add the butternut squash and toss, add the varbecue sauce and give everything a good mix.

Plate up and garnish with red chilli slices and toasted sesame seeds.

✸ **This dish would be a great sharing side to your main meal, or why not have it as your main meal by adding rice or noodles?**

nasi goreng

A super tasty and quick to make fried rice dish popular in Indonesia and Malaysia.

serves 2

150g (5oz) long grain white rice
100g (3½oz) green beans
2 tablespoons kecap manis
1 tablespoon soy sauce
3 tablespoons vegetable oil
2 garlic cloves, crushed
1 large red fresh chilli, sliced
1 carrot, peeled and sliced
6 shiitake mushrooms, sliced
1 large shallot, chopped
120g (4oz) beef fillet, sliced thinly into batons
3 free-range eggs
2 sprigs of coriander

Cook the rice according to the packet instructions. This will make roughly 300g (10oz) cooked rice.

Blanch the beans by plunging them into boiling water for 2–3 minutes so they still have a crunch, then cool under cold running water and cut in half.

In a small bowl, mix together the kecap manis and soy sauce.

Place a wok over a high heat, add the oil, then the garlic and chilli, quickly followed by the beans, carrot, mushrooms, shallot and beef. Stir-fry for 2–3 minutes.

Whisk 1 egg, add to the wok and, as it starts to cook, add the rice, tossing and mixing everything together.

In a separate frying pan, fry the remaining 2 eggs until crispy at the edges.

Now add two-thirds of the sauce to the wok and mix in for 30 seconds. Remove from the heat and spoon into bowls.

Top each with a fried egg, drizzle over the remaining sauce and garnish with coriander.

✴ **Replace the beef with a vegan substitute for a delicious vegetarian nasi goreng.**

✴ **If you can't find kecap manis, use a bit of Worcestershire sauce and add a touch of sugar to your soy sauce.**

✴ **To save time, you can use pre-cooked packet rice in this dish.**

lamb mokutan

This dish takes longer to make, but it's worth the wait. Slow-cooked and tender, with a citrus-flavoured soy

serves 2

2 teaspoons ginger paste

2 teaspoons garlic paste

1¾ teaspoons salt

20g (¾oz) mint leaves, finely chopped

½kg (1lb 2oz) bone-in lamb shoulder

300g (10oz) charcoal noodles

2 tablespoons vegetable oil

2 pak choi, leaves separated

1 medium-size red onion, finely sliced

40g (1½oz) mangetout, sliced lengthways into thin strips

4 spring onions, topped, tailed and sliced at an angle

2 tablespoons teriyaki sauce (see page 177)

90ml (3fl oz) citrus ponzu sauce (see page 172)

2.5cm (1in) piece of ginger, julienned

a few sprigs of mint, leaves picked

Prepare your lamb for marinating the day before or on the morning of your evening meal. In a mixing bowl, place the ginger and garlic pastes, salt and chopped mint leaves and mix well. Rub the marinade all over the lamb shoulder, then refrigerate for at least 6 hours (the longer it marinates, the better the flavour).

Preheat the oven to 160°C/325°F/gas mark 3. Place the marinated lamb shoulder on a lightly oiled roasting tray, cover with foil and cook in the oven for 4 hours.

Remove the lamb from the oven and set aside to rest for a couple of hours. Using a fork, shred the lamb meat off the bone. Measure out 200g (7oz) and refrigerate the rest for later.

Cook the charcoal noodles, following the packet instructions, then cool under cold running water to stop them cooking. Drain and set aside.

Place a wok or large pan over a high heat, warm the oil and stir-fry the pak choi, red onion, mangetout and spring onion. Lower the heat to medium, add the cooked noodles and keep tossing until heated through. Add the teriyaki sauce and toss until everything is thoroughly coated, then take off the heat.

In a separate small pan, add 200g (7oz) of the cooked lamb and reheat. Once hot, add the citrus ponzu sauce and stir well.

Spoon the lamb on top of the noodles and garnish with ginger and mint leaves. If you have any excess lamb, why not use it on a salad or in some bao buns.

miso chicken harusame

Using a lighter noodle and packed full of veg, this dish is based on a Japanese salad recipe but is served up hot.

serves 2

1 teaspoon garlic paste
1 teaspoon white miso paste
1 teaspoon tamari sauce
2 chicken breast fillets, cut into 1cm (½in) thick slices
30g (1oz) curly kale, destalked
80g (3oz) pak choi, leaves separated
1 tablespoon vegetable oil
80g (3oz) rice glass bean noodles
1 medium-size red pepper, thinly sliced
1 medium-size red onion, thinly sliced
50g (2oz) shiitake mushrooms, destalked and sliced
4 red chillies, sliced
2 sprigs of coriander, leaves picked
1 teaspoon chilli oil

for the sauce
2 teaspoons tamari sauce
2 teaspoons white miso paste
2 teaspoons fish sauce
1 tablespoon water
1 teaspoon chilli oil

In a bowl, whisk together the garlic paste, miso paste and tamari sauce, ensuring there are no lumps. Add the chicken slices, turning and coating them in the marinade, then set aside for a minimum of 30 minutes.

Measure all the sauce ingredients into a bowl, mix well until you have a smooth consistency, then set aside for later.

Next, prepare the veg: shred the curly kale into small pieces and cut any large pak choi leaves into two. Mix all the vegetables together, ready for stir-frying.

Place an oiled wok on a medium–high heat, add the marinated chicken and cook for about 3–5 minutes until starting to brown.

Meanwhile, cook the glass bean noodles, following the packet instructions. Once cooked, drain and set aside.

Add the prepped vegetables to the chicken and stir fry for a few minutes until caramelised. Add half of the sauce and coat all of the ingredients. Then add your noodles and toss, followed by the rest of the sauce and stir well.

Plate up into bowls and garnish with sliced chilli and coriander. For an extra kick, finish with a couple of drops of chilli oil.

✸ **Use 200g (7oz) fried tofu instead of chicken and remove the fish sauce to make this dish vegan.**

flexible favourites

We're passionate about plant-based food at wagamama, and we believe meat free shouldn't mean taste free. There are no second-thought, token veggie options in this chapter: only plant-based heroes and powerhouse proteins designed to nourish your body and mind. Even if you're not vegan or even veg curious, we bet there's a bowl in here for you.

Firecracker tofu, vegan chilli squid, a plant-based donburi and the iconic vegatsu. All vegan. All delicious.

The world could do with everyone eating a little less meat and a little more veg. This chapter is designed to help you do just that. The wagamama way.

vegan chilli squid

A wagamama classic, now vegan. Made with king oyster mushrooms that resemble the texture of squid.

serves 2

300g (10oz) king oyster mushrooms (about 4), sliced lengthways into 'chips'
30g (1oz) chickpea flour
30ml (1fl oz) sticky vegan sauce (see page 169)
100g (3½oz) plain flour
a pinch of bicarbonate of soda
310ml (10fl oz) vegetable oil
2 teaspoons shichimi powder

First wash and drain the oyster mushrooms, making sure a little moisture is left on them, then roll and toss in the chickpea flour and set aside.

Make sure the sticky vegan sauce is ready to hand for later.

To make the batter, sift the flour with the bicarbonate of soda into a mixing bowl. In a separate bowl, mix together 10ml (2 teaspoons) oil with 175ml (6 fl oz) water, then gradually add this to the flour, whisking gently to ensure there are no lumps.

Pour the remaining vegetable oil into a deep pan and place over a medium heat. Add one drop of batter to see if the oil is ready; the batter should sizzle and not drop to the bottom of the pan.

Using a chopstick, pick up one of the mushroom pieces, drop in the batter and turn to ensure it is coated all over, then place into the oil and cook until light golden in colour. Repeat with all the mushroom and all the batter and, when each piece is cooked, lift out of the pan and transfer to a plate lined with kitchen paper to get rid of any excess oil.

Arrange all the battered mushroom in a mixing bowl and sprinkle with shichimi powder to coat all the pieces.

Transfer to a serving plate with a ramekin of sticky vegan sauce.

wagamama your way

yasai katsu hot

Our vegan classic, spiced up.

serves 2

300ml kastu curry sauce (see page 177)
1 tablespoon firecracker sauce (see page 176)
2 tablespoons wagamama dressing (see page 178)
150g (5oz) sticky rice, cooked (see page 178)
50g (2oz) plain flour
1 medium-size aubergine, sliced into 4 thick pieces
1 small sweet potato, peeled and sliced into 4 thick pieces
100g (3½oz) panko breadcrumbs
1 teaspoon chilli oil
a pinch of chilli flakes
1 tablespoon sriracha sauce
150ml (5fl oz) vegetable oil, for deep-frying
80g (3oz) mixed salad leaves
2 tablespoons Japanese pickles

First make your katsu sauce, firecracker sauce and wagamama dressing as per the recipes and set aside for later.

Cook the rice, then divide between two serving plates and keep warm.

In a bowl, whisk together the plain flour with a splash of vegetable oil, ensuring there are no lumps. Add water until the consistency is in between single and double cream; this is your batter.

Dip the aubergine and sweet potato pieces in the batter, allowing any excess to drip off, then place them in the panko breadcrumbs, making sure each is coated evenly all over.

In a saucepan, place the katsu sauce and mix in the chilli oil, chilli flakes, sriracha sauce and firecracker sauce to get a fiery version of our legendary katsu curry sauce. Gently heat and bring to a simmer. Keep warm.

Place the oil in a deep pan over a medium heat. To test if the oil is ready for frying, drop a couple of breadcrumbs into the oil; if they don't sizzle the oil is not hot enough and if they burn then the oil is too hot – they should bubble and float to the top. When the right temperature, deep-fry the panko aubergine and sweet potato steaks, one at a time, until golden brown (about 2–3 minutes on each side). Transfer to a plate lined with kitchen paper to remove any excess oil.

Arrange the panko aubergine and sweet potato over the rice and drizzle the hot katsu sauce all over the dish. Place salad leaves on the side and drizzle each plate with 1 tablespoon of salad dressing. Garnish with Japanese pickles and serve.

✶ **If you don't fancy the heat, leave out the firecracker sauce, sriracha and chilli flakes to make our normal katsu curry sauce. You could even use our off-the-shelf katsu paste if you don't want to make yours from scratch.**

yasai itame

A vegan, fragrant, coconut curried soup – a hug in a bowl.

serves 2

600ml (20fl oz) coconut + ginger sauce
(see page 176)

2 small pak choi, leaves picked and tough
parts of stalks removed

200g (7oz) rice stick noodles

1 tablespoon vegetable oil (for frying)

250g (9oz) firm tofu, cut into 2.5cm (1in)
cubes

50g (2oz) shiitake mushrooms, finely
sliced and stalks removed

1 medium red pepper, sliced

1 medium red onion, sliced

2 spring onions, cut into 2.5cm (1in)
pieces

100g (3½oz) beansprouts, rinsed and
drained

to garnish

1 teaspoon toasted coconut chips

4–5 mint leaves, finely sliced

a small handful of coriander, leaves picked

1 small red chilli, finely sliced

½ lime, cut into 2 wedges

Make the coconut + ginger sauce according to the recipe on page 176, and, while it is cooking, prepare the rest of the dish. Cut any big leaves of the pak choi in half and set aside. Cook the rice stick noodles according to the packet instructions, then drain and divide between two bowls.

Place a wok or a wide-based pan over a medium heat and add the oil. Once hot, add the tofu cubes and cook until they start to brown. Add the shiitake mushrooms, red pepper, red onion, pak choi leaves, spring onions and beansprouts. Stir fry for about 2 minutes until the vegetables start to soften.

Add the coconut + ginger sauce and heat until the sauce is starting to boil, then turn down the heat and simmer for 5 minutes. This is your itame mix.

Pour a small amount of the sauce over the noodles and loosen the noodles with chopsticks. Then pour the rest of the itame mix over the noodles, ensuring you divide the sauce, vegetables and tofu equally between the bowls.

Garnish with the coconut chips, mint, coriander leaves, red chilli and lime wedges and serve.

yasai pad thai

Our take on a Thai classic, made vegan.

serves 2

150g (5oz) firm tofu, cut into 2.5cm (1in) cubes
2 teaspoons vegetable oil
200g (7oz) rice stick noodles
2.5cm (1in) piece of ginger, finely chopped
1 garlic clove, finely chopped
½ leek, finely sliced
1 medium-size red onion, finely sliced
4 spring onions, topped, tailed, sliced in half lengthwise and chopped into 2.5cm (1in) pieces
200g (7oz) beansprouts
1 small red chilli, finely sliced
a pinch of chilli flakes
100ml (3½fl oz) amai sauce (see page 176)
a few sprigs of coriander, leaves picked
a few sprigs of mint, leaves picked and finely sliced
5g (1 teaspoon) fried shallots
2 limes, cut into wedges
1 teaspoon nibbed peanuts

Place the rice noodles in a saucepan and cover with boiling water. Leave for 5 minutes, or until the noodles are cooked, then drain and wash under cold running water. Drizzle with a teaspoon of oil, toss and set aside.

Heat a teaspoon of oil in a wok or wide-based pan over a high heat and add the tofu to brown evenly on each side. Then add your chopped ginger, garlic and then all the vegetables, chilli slices and chilli flakes and stir-fry, ensuring the veg is starting to take on a nice colour.

Reduce the heat, add the rice noodles and cook, then add the amai sauce and give everything a mix (being careful not to break the noodles). Simmer to allow the sauce to reduce slightly so that it becomes sticky and coats the noodles.

Serve the pad Thai on plates garnished with coriander, mint, fried shallots, a lime wedge and nibbed peanuts.

★ **Why not use our off-the-shelf pad Thai sauce instead of making your own?**

no-duck donburi

A vegan version of our famous duck donburi, using a cherry hoisin sauce to give a warming spicy sweetness.

serves 2

125g (4½oz) brown sticky rice, cooked (see page 178)

60g (2oz) edamame beans

2 tablespoons vegetable oil

50g (2oz) shiitake mushrooms, destalked and finely sliced

1 x 150g (5oz) seitan steak, sliced into long, thin strips

90ml (3fl oz) spicy cherry hoisin sauce (see page 172)

80g (3oz) vegan kimchee

½ cucumber, julienned

4 spring onions, topped, tailed and sliced at an angle

a few sprigs of coriander, leaves picked

1 red chilli, finely sliced

First cook the rice, then divide between two serving bowls and keep the rice warm and fluffy.

Next, prepare the edamame beans: blanch them in boiling water for 2 minutes, then plunge into ice-cold water, drain and set aside.

Place the oil in a medium-size pan over a medium heat and gently stir-fry the mushrooms with the shredded seitan for two minutes. The seitan should crisp up and the mushrooms should lightly caramelise – ensure you do not break the seitan into small pieces. Add three-quarters of the cherry hoisin sauce, mix well, then take the pan off the heat.

Take the two serving bowls with brown rice and spoon the stir-fry on top. Add the edamame beans, vegan kimchee, cucumber and spring onion, then drizzle over the remaining cherry hoisin sauce. Garnish with coriander and sliced red chilli and serve.

✱ Seitan is growing in popularity as a meat substitute and is made from gluten, the main protein in wheat.

kinoko donburi

The mix of rice, vegetables and Japanese-inspired flavours makes for a nourishing bowl of goodness. 'Kinoko' means mushroom in Japanese.

serves 2

2 tablespoons sticky vegan sauce (see page 169)

2 tablespoons teriyaki sauce (see page 177)

2 tablespoons yakitori sauce (see page 177)

200g (7oz) brown sticky rice, cooked (see page 178)

60g (2oz) edamame beans

1 tablespoon oil

200g (7oz) mixed mushrooms, thinly sliced

50g (2oz) cherry tomatoes, cut in half

20g (¾oz) pea shoots

80g (3oz) vegan kimchee (see page 179)

4 spring onions, topped, tailed and sliced at an angle

1 teaspoon mixed sesame seeds

Ensure all of your sauces are prepared so you can add them straight into the stir fry later on. First cook the rice, then divide between two serving bowls and cover to keep warm.

Next, prepare the edamame beans: blanch them in boiling water for 2 minutes, then plunge into ice-cold water, drain and set aside.

Place the oil in a medium-size pan over a medium heat and stir-fry the mushrooms for a minute before adding the edamame beans and cherry tomatoes. Give everything a good stir until the mushrooms are completely cooked, then add the sticky vegan sauce and mix well again.

Take the two serving bowls and fluff up the rice with a fork. Drizzle equal quantities of teriyaki and yakitori sauce all over the brown rice. Arrange the stir-fried veg on one side of the rice, then add the pea shoots, vegan kimchee and spring onions on the other side. Garnish with sesame seeds and serve.

✴ **You could use our wagamama teriyaki sauce from the supermarket to save time on preparation for this sauce.**

yasai yaki soba

This dish translates as vegetable fried noodles. A staple on the wagamama menu and loved by our vegan and non-vegan guests.

serves 2

300g (10oz) rice stick noodles
2 tablespoons vegetable oil
40g (1½oz) shiitake mushrooms, sliced
40g (1½oz) closed cup mushrooms, sliced
½ green pepper, sliced
½ red pepper, sliced
2 spring onions, finely sliced
200g (7oz) beansprouts
1 small red onion, finely sliced
1 teaspoon garlic paste
2 tablespoons soy sauce

to garnish
2 tablespoons spicy vinegar (see page 178)
20g (¾oz) pickled ginger
1 teaspoon fried shallots
1 teaspoon toasted mixed sesame seeds

Place the rice noodles in a saucepan and cover with boiling water. Leave for 5 minutes or until the noodles are cooked. Drain and wash under cold running water. Drizzle with a teaspoon of oil, toss and set aside.

Heat the oil over a medium–high heat in a wok or a large pan. Once hot, add all the vegetables, garlic paste and drained noodles.

Quickly toss the ingredients, making sure the oil coats the noodles well. Cook for 3–4 minutes, keeping the ingredients moving in the wok or pan.

Add the soy sauce and toss again, making sure that the sauce does not stick to the wok.

Once all the ingredients are piping hot and the vegetables are cooked but still have some bite to them, divide between two plates.

Garnish with the spicy vinegar, pickled ginger, shallots and sesame seeds.

✶ **If you aren't vegan, you could add 2 whisked eggs when you are cooking the vegetables, and swap the rice noodles for egg noodles. This is how an authentic Japanese yaki soba would be made.**

tofu firecracker

A vegan version of our restaurant classic. If you like spice, this is the dish for you.

serves 2

250g (9oz) firm tofu, cut into 2.5cm (1in) cubes
150g (5oz) jasmine rice
2 tablespoons vegetable oil, for frying
8 spring onions, topped and tailed
2 teaspoons ginger paste
2 teaspoons garlic paste
6 long dried chillies, finely chopped
1 medium-size white onion, finely sliced
1 small red pepper, sliced into 2.5cm (1in) dice
1 small green pepper, sliced into 2.5cm (1in) dice
50g (2oz) mangetout, topped and tailed
180ml (6fl oz) firecracker sauce (see page 176)
½ lime, cut into 2 wedges
½ teaspoon shichimi powder
a few drops of sesame oil

Take six of the spring onions, slice them in half lengthwise and cut into 2.5cm (1in) pieces.

Cook the rice according to the packet instructions, then divide between two serving plates and keep warm.

Heat the 2 tablespoons of oil in a wok or large frying pan and cook the tofu until it turns golden brown on each side. Then add the ginger and garlic pastes and dried chillies and give a quick stir, then add the rest of the vegetables and keep stirring over a high heat. Once the tofu is hot, add the firecracker sauce, toss and stir well.

Spoon the stir fry onto the plate and garnish with lime and the remaining spring onions, finely chopped. Sprinkle a little shichimi powder over the rice and finish with a drizzle of sesame oil.

✷ **For a super-quick meal, you could buy our wagamama firecracker sauce from a supermarket to make this dish.**

tofu chilli men

A classic dish that was loved by our guests for many years, now made vegan using tofu.

serves 2

250g (9oz) firm tofu, cut into 2.5cm (1in) cubes

150ml (5fl oz) vegetable oil (for frying the tofu)

150g (5oz) soba noodles

30ml (1fl oz) vegetable oil

1 carrot, cut into 1cm (½in) cubes

½ courgette, cut into 2.5cm (1in) thick cubes

1 small red onion, sliced into 3mm (⅛in) slices

4 spring onions, cut into 2.5cm (1in) pieces

60g (2oz) mangetout, sliced

500ml (18fl oz) chilli men sauce (see page 176)

medium tomato, cut into 8 pieces

Heat the oil in a frying pan and once hot, fry the tofu cubes until golden. Remove with a slotted spoon and transfer to another plate lined with kitchen paper to drain any excess oil.

Cook the soba noodles according to the packet instructions. Divide between two serving bowls, keeping the noodles to one side.

Place a wok pan on a medium heat and add the oil. Once hot, add the carrots, courgettes, onion, spring onion and mangetout and toss, then reduce the heat and add the tofu.

Add the chilli men sauce, then turn the heat down. Add the tomato and cook until the sauce simmers. Remove from the heat.

Add the tofu, vegetables and sauce to the opposite side of the bowl to the noodles.

tofu kare lomen

A spicy coconut soup, based on a classic laksa recipe.

serves 2

500ml (18fl oz) kare lomen sauce (see page 167)
150g (5oz) beansprouts
20g (¾oz) cornflour
½ pack (150g/5oz) silken tofu, cut into 8 cubes
100ml (3½fl oz) vegetable oil, for frying
2 x 125g (4½oz) vegan ramen noodles
½ cucumber, julienned
a few sprigs of coriander, leaves picked
½ lime, cut into 2 wedges

First prepare the kare lomen sauce and have it in the pan, gently simmering and ready to go for later.

Blanch the beansprouts in boiling water for 30 seconds, then drain and set aside.

Place the cornflour in a shallow dish and coat the tofu cubes all over.

Heat the oil in a frying pan and, once hot, fry the tofu cubes until golden. Remove with a slotted spoon and transfer to a plate lined with kitchen paper to soak up any excess oil.

Place the noodles in a saucepan and cook according to the instructions on the packet. Divide between two serving bowls and use chopsticks to separate the noodles so they don't stick.

Pile the beansprouts on top of the noodles and the cucumber and pour over the hot kare lomen sauce. Add four pieces of fried silken tofu to each bowl, garnish with coriander and a lime wedge and serve.

hot vegatsu

A vegan favourite from our restaurant menu.

serves 2

300ml katsu curry sauce (see page 177)
1 tablespoon firecracker sauce (see page 176)
2 tablespoons wagamama dressing (see page 178)
150g (5oz) sticky rice, cooked (see page 178)
50g (2oz) plain flour
150ml (5fl oz) vegetable oil, for deep-frying
2 seitan steaks
100g (3½oz) panko breadcrumbs
1 teaspoon chilli oil
a pinch of chilli flakes
1 tablespoon sriracha sauce
80g (3oz) mixed salad leaves
2 tablespoons Japanese pickles

First make your katsu sauce, firecracker sauce and wagamama dressing, following the recipes, and set aside for later.

Cook the rice, then divide between two serving plates and keep warm.

In a bowl, whisk together the plain flour with a splash of vegetable oil, ensuring there are no lumps. Add water until the consistency is in between single and double cream; this is your batter.

Dip the seitan steaks in the batter, allowing any excess to drip off, then roll them in the panko breadcrumbs, making sure each is coated evenly all over.

In a saucepan, place the katsu sauce and mix in the chilli oil, chilli flakes, sriracha sauce and firecracker sauce to get a fiery version of our legendary katsu curry sauce. Gently heat and bring to a simmer. Keep warm.

Place the oil in a deep pan over a medium heat. To test if the oil is ready for frying, drop a couple of breadcrumbs into the oil; if they don't sizzle the oil is not hot enough and if they burn then the oil is too hot – they should bubble and float to the top. When the right temperature, deep-fry the seitan steaks, one at a time, until golden brown (about 2–3 minutes on each side). Transfer to a plate lined with kitchen paper to remove any excess oil.

Slice the panko seitan into thick strips and arrange over the rice, and drizzle the hot katsu sauce all over the dish. Place salad leaves on the side and drizzle each plate with 1 tablespoon of salad dressing. Garnish with Japanese pickles and serve.

✦ **If you don't fancy the heat, just use our normal katsu sauce and don't add the chilli oil, chilli flakes, sriracha and firecracker.**

5

something sweet

There's always room for dessert, and we made sure to make extra. In this chapter you'll find sweet treats dipped and drizzled in the flavours of the East.

Inspired by the unique ingredients of Asia, these classic desserts have been given the wagamama treatment. Think deep-fried bao, saucy gyozas and the beloved banana katsu. Dish up one of these desserts and end things on a high note.

If you're feeling parched, we've got you covered. Flick through to find fresh juices and Asian-inspired cocktails. Sip on nourishmint or savour a sweet lychee cocktail. With easy swaps, these drinks can be made your way.

banana katsu

Fried bananas with a katsu crunch and toffee sauce… irresistible.

serves 2

50g (2oz) plain flour
150ml (5fl oz) vegetable oil, for frying
40g (1½oz) panko breadcrumbs
2 bananas, sliced in half
2 scoops salted caramel ice cream

for the toffee sauce
20g (¾oz) vegan butter
1 heaped tablespoon sugar
2 tablespoons coconut milk
a pinch of sea salt

Start by making the toffee sauce. Place the vegan butter and sugar in a saucepan (non-stick) over a medium heat and stir until it starts to turn an amber colour. Carefully pour in the coconut milk; it will be bubbly but just continue to whisk continuously. Cook until the sauce thickens, adding salt to taste. Set aside and keep warm.

In a bowl, whisk together the plain flour with a splash of oil, ensuring there are no lumps. Add a tablespoon of water at a time until the consistency is between single and double cream; this is your batter.

Place the panko breadcrumbs in a shallow bowl. Dunk the bananas into the vegan batter and then roll them in the breadcrumbs.

Place the oil in a deep saucepan over a medium heat. To test if the oil is ready; drop a couple of breadcrumbs into the oil. If they don't sizzle the oil is not hot enough, if they burn then the oil is too hot – they should bubble and float to the top.

Carefully lower the panko bananas into the oil and cook until golden. Remove with a slotted spoon, drain off the excess oil and place two halves in each bowl.

Add a scoop of ice cream to each bowl and drizzle with toffee sauce.

✸ If you're not vegan, just use the same quantities of normal butter and cream instead of coconut milk.

✸ We love the Northern Bloc Salted Caramel and Almond Swirl Ice Cream.

soufflé
pancakes

Beautifully light, fluffy pancakes. wagamama's easier version of traditional Japanese soufflé pancakes.

serves 2

30g (1oz) unsalted butter
3 free-range eggs, separated
50g (2oz) caster sugar
80g (3oz) self-raising flour
1 teaspoon baking powder
a pinch of salt
½ tsp lemon juice
2 teaspoons vegetable oil

topping ideas
yuzu marmalade (see page 27)
raspberry compote (see page 27)
fruit + ice cream
strawberries + cream
banana + toffee sauce (see page 146)
icing sugar

Warm the butter in the microwave until it has just melted.

In a mixing bowl, whisk the egg yolks with the melted butter and half the caster sugar until frothy. Sift in the flour, baking powder and salt, and mix to form a thick batter.

In a separate bowl, add the remaining caster sugar, egg whites and lemon juice and whisk until the egg whites are stiff and glossy.

Add a couple of spoonfuls of the egg white mixture to the thick batter, and mix to loosen the batter. Fold the rest of the whites into the batter. Make sure you do this very gently to keep as much air in the mixture as possible. This will ensure that your pancakes are light and fluffy.

Heat a lightly oiled frying pan (with a lid) on a very low heat. Add two dollops of the mixture to the pan and cover with the lid. This will help keep the heat in the pan and cook the pancakes through.

After 2–3 minutes the pancakes will have started to set. Using a spatula, carefully flip one pancake on top of the other, with the uncooked sides together. You will now have one tall pancake. Cook for another 30–60 seconds until fully cooked. Repeat to make one more tall pancake.

Garnish with a topping of your choice. We used a dollop of yuzu marmalade, a handful of raspberries and icing sugar.

sweet gyoza

Because gyozas don't always have to be savoury.

serves 2

10 gyoza skins (see page 181) or buy frozen from a Chinese supermarket
100ml (3½fl oz) vegetable oil, for shallow-frying

chocolate + coconut filling
3 tablespoons desiccated coconut
150g (5oz) milk or dark chocolate, broken into squares

apple + raspberry filling
1 apple, peeled, cored and cubed
2 tablespoons sugar
½ punnet of raspberries

banana, peanut butter + chocolate hazelnut filling
1 banana
1 tablespoon peanut butter
1 tablespoon chocolate hazelnut spread

If you have frozen gyoza skins, let them defrost completely before starting. Keep your gyoza skins covered so that they don't dry out.

Place your gyoza skins on a flat surface and spoon a small amount of your chosen filling into the middle of each piece (ensure you don't add too much, otherwise you won't be able to fold).

Dip your finger in a little water and run it around the edge of the gyoza – this will help the gyoza stick when you fold.

Lift the bottom of the gyoza and fold it over the filling to meet the top edge of the gyoza. Pinch and fold the two sides together, ensuring you have a flat bottom.

Refrigerate the filled gyozas to allow them to set and rest.

When you are ready, heat the oil in a pan over a medium–high heat and shallow-fry until golden.

Transfer to a bowl, toss with a little sugar, and even a little ginger or cinnamon. Or dust with a mix of matcha powder and icing sugar and enjoy!

chocolate + coconut
Melt the chocolate in a saucepan over a very low heat, add the desiccated coconut and stir until the chocolate takes on a gritty texture and holds together well.

apple + raspberry
Place the apple in a saucepan with the sugar and cook over a low heat until the apples are soft.

Remove from the heat and stir in the raspberries. Once cooled, your mix is ready to use.

banana, peanut butter + chocolate hazelnut
Mash the banana into a bowl, add the peanut butter and chocolate hazelnut spread and mix to combine.

✦ **Why not make mince pie gyozas at Christmas time, using your favourite fruit mincemeat?**

wagamama your way

baonut

serves 2

2 bao buns (see page 180) or buy from
  an Asian supermarket
100ml (3½fl oz) vegetable oil, for
  deep-frying
¾ tablespoon caster sugar
2 scoops of ice cream
70g (3oz) mixed fruit

for the toffee sauce
20ml (⅔oz) butter
20g (¾oz) sugar
20ml cream
a pinch of sea salt

other ideas
chocolate hazelnut spread + banana
raspberry compote + cream
banana katsu
bacon + maple syrup
custard
cinnamon sugar

First make the bao buns, following the recipe on page 180.

Start by making the toffee sauce. Place the butter and sugar in a saucepan (non-stick) over a medium heat and stir until it starts to turn an amber colour. Carefully pour in the cream; it will be bubbly but just continue to whisk continuously. Cook until the sauce thickens, adding salt to taste. Set aside and keep warm.

Place the oil in a saucepan over a medium heat and fry the bao buns on both sides until golden brown. Transfer to a plate lined with kitchen paper to soak up any excess oil.

Spread the caster sugar out onto a plate and roll the baonuts in the sugar until they are fully coated.

Serve your baonuts in a bowl with two scoops of ice cream, and mixed fruits of your choice. Drizzle over toffee sauce and enjoy!

✱ **You could pick up some ready-made bao buns from an Asian speciality store, or they are even becoming more readily available in supermarkets too.**

juices/smoothies

high five

serves 1

½ lemon, peeled and cut into chunks

2 green apples, cored and sliced

60ml (2fl oz) fresh orange juice

75g (3oz) melon, deseeded and cut into chunks

75g (3oz) pineapple, cut into chunks

ice cubes (if making a smoothie)

Put all the ingredients through a juicer, then decant into a large glass and enjoy.

If you don't have a juicer, add the fruit to a blender with ice and blitz away until you have a smoothie texture, adding more ice if necessary.

....

✴ If you don't want to have to prep the melon and pineapple, why not buy a pack of pre-prepped from the chilled section of the supermarket?

up beet

serves 1

4 green apples, cored and cubed

10cm (4in)-long piece of cucumber, cubed

15g (½oz) red pepper, cubed

50g (2oz) cooked beetroot, peeled and cubed

1cm (½in) piece of fresh ginger, peeled and cubed

ice cubes (if making a smoothie)

Put all of the ingredients through a juicer, then decant into a large glass and enjoy.

However, if you don't have a juicer or prefer a smoothie, place all the ingredients with ice in a blender and blitz away until you have a smoothie texture (add more ice if necessary), then decant into a glass and enjoy.

....

✴ Be careful with the beetroot as it may stain!

nourishmint

serves 1

½ lemon, peeled and cut into chunks

3 green apples, cored and cut into chunks

8g (¼oz) fresh mint leaves

ice cubes (if making a smoothie)

Put all the ingredients through a juicer, then decant into a large glass and enjoy.

If you don't have a juicer, add the fruit to a blender with ice and blitz away until you have a smoothie texture, adding more ice if necessary.

cocktails

elderflower + ginger

serves 1

25ml (½fl oz) elderflower syrup
25ml (½fl oz) lemon juice
200ml (7fl oz) ginger ale
a few sprigs of mint, to garnish

Place all the ingredients in a highball glass and gently stir to combine.

Garnish with a sprig of mint, and enjoy!

ginger citrus

serves 1

35ml (1fl oz) your favourite whisky
1 tablespoon Cointreau
3 dashes of orange bitters

25ml (½fl oz) Ginger Syrup (see page 173)
25ml (½fl oz) lemon juice
10g fresh ginger, peeled and sliced, to garnish

Place all the ingredients in a rocks glass over ice and stir.

Garnish with a slice of fresh ginger and enjoy!

sweet lychee

serves 1

35ml (1fl oz) your favourite vodka
25ml (½fl oz) lychee liqueur
25ml (½fl oz) lemon juice
75ml (3fl oz) pineapple juice
1 sprig of mint, to garnish

Place all the ingredients in a cocktail shaker with ice and shake well.

Strain into a short glass over ice, garnish with sprig of fresh mint and enjoy.

✶ Fun fact: pineapple juice in drinks gives you the foam that you'd usually only see in cocktails that use egg white – a great vegan alternative!

yuzu kick

serves 1

1 small red chilli
35ml (1fl oz) your favourite gin
1 tablespoon yuzu sake or yuzu liquor
25ml (½fl oz) lemon juice

12.5ml (¼fl oz) sugar syrup (see below)
125ml (4fl oz) soda water
a sprig of mint, to garnish

Slice the chilli lengthways. Keep one half for a garnish and remove the seeds from the other half and slice into 3–4 pieces.

Place all the remaining ingredients, including the sliced chilli, in a highball glass with ice and gently stir.

Garnish with fresh chilli on the glass and a sprig of mint, and enjoy!

✶ You can buy sugar syrup from a shop or make it at home – dissolve 100g (3½oz) sugar in 50ml (2fl oz) water and simmer over a low heat, then cool and store in the fridge for use in your next cocktail.

6.

sauces + sides

Sauce has the power to take a dish from good to great with one simple stir. Dollop, dunk, mix or marinade. Whatever you do, it's all in the sauce.

This chapter will teach you how to blend and bottle some of our most legendary sauces and dressings. Plus, stir up some saucy new flavours you won't find on the bench. Vegan sambal, shiok marinade, Korean red curry and chilli men. Once you master our not-so-secret sauces, you can make just about anything taste good.

And what's a sauce, without a side for it to go on? You'll also find how-tos for some sauce-able sides including hirata buns and vegan kimchee.

kare lomen sauce

A spicy yet zesty sauce – our take on a classic laksa, but vegan.

serves 2 (makes 500g/1lb 2oz)

1 medium-size red pepper, cubed

½ medium-size red onion, cubed

1 garlic clove, finely chopped

2 lemongrass stalks, finely chopped

2.5cm (1in) piece of galangal, chopped

1 tablespoon hot curry paste

2 tablespoons madras curry powder

1 tablespoon chilli powder

1 teaspoon ground turmeric

1 teaspoon ground fennel

100ml (3fl oz) chilli oil

1 x 400ml (14fl oz) can coconut milk (but add more for a really creamy sauce)

a pinch or two of salt

1 teaspoon caster sugar

Place all the vegetables, garlic and spices in a food processor or blender and blitz to a fine paste.

Place the chilli oil in a saucepan over a low heat and, once the oil warms up, add your paste and cook, stirring, for a good 20–30 minutes – the longer the better to let all that amazing flavour come out.

Add 200ml (7fl oz) water to the pan and bring to the boil. Add the coconut milk, salt and sugar and simmer for around 5–6 minutes until you can see oil releasing around the sides.

Take off the heat and allow to cool before transferring to a lidded container. Store in the refrigerator.

✹ If you can't find galangal, you can just use ginger.

✹ The way to prepare lemongrass stalks is to smash them first (using the back of a knife), before you chop.

korean red curry sauce [1]

makes 500ml (18fl oz)

60ml (2fl oz) vegetable oil

3–4 garlic cloves, finely
    chopped

5cm (2in) piece ginger, peeled
    and finely chopped

1 tablespoon lemongrass paste

½ teaspoon red chilli powder

2 tablespoons gochujang paste

300ml (10fl oz) vegetable stock

1 tablespoon tamarind paste

125ml (4fl oz) coconut milk

1 tablespoon cornflour

a pinch of salt

1 teaspoon sugar

Place a heavy-bottomed deep saucepan over a medium
heat, add the oil, garlic, ginger and lemongrass and
sauté until light golden brown, then add the chilli powder
and gochujang paste, reduce the heat and cook for
a further minute.

Add the vegetable stock and tamarind paste and bring to a
boil, then reduce the heat, add the coconut milk and bring
to a simmer.

In a small bowl, mix the cornflour with a teaspoon of water
to make a thick paste. Whisk to ensure there are no lumps.

Slowly add the cornflour paste to the sauce, mixing all the
time. Cook until the sauce becomes the consistency of
double cream. Add the salt and sugar, mix again and then
take off the heat.

Allow to cool before transferring to a lidded container and
store in the refrigerator.

sticky vegan sauce [2]

makes 200ml (7fl oz)

50ml (2fl oz) amai sauce
    (see page 176)

2 tablespoons chilli katsu
    sauce (see page 177)

2 tablespoons spicy vinegar
    (see page 178)

2 tablespoons soy sauce

Place all the ingredients in a large bowl and whisk until all
combined.

Transfer to a lidded container or jar and store in the fridge.

varbecue sauce [3]

makes 300ml (10fl oz)

180ml (7fl oz) amai sauce
    (see page 176)

45ml (2fl oz) soy sauce

90ml (3fl oz) sriracha sauce

Measure all the ingredients into a bowl and whisk well,
then decant into a lidded container and store in the
refrigerator.

wagamama vegan sambal

makes 350ml (12fl oz)

1 x 400g (14oz) tin whole
   plum tomatoes
1 red pepper, roughly chopped
1 lemongrass stalk, crushed
   and chopped
2–3 garlic cloves
2 chillies, destalked

2 tablespoons vegetable oil
1 tablespoon chilli oil
1 tablespoon chilli powder
1½ tablespoons gochujang
   paste
a pinch of salt

Take 2–3 tomatoes from the tin and drain the excess juice.
Place in a food processor or blender with the pepper,
lemongrass, garlic and chilli and blitz.

Transfer to a saucepan, add the oil and chilli oil, and warm
over a low heat, cooking for 5 minutes.

Add the chilli powder and cook for 30 seconds, then add
gochujang paste and cook, stirring occasionally, for 25–30
minutes. You will see the oil releasing on the side of the pan.

Take the pan off the heat, add the salt and allow to cool.
Transfer to a lidded container or jar and store in the fridge.

....

korean bbq sauce

makes 150ml (5fl oz)

60ml (2fl oz) bulgogi sauce
20ml (⅔fl oz) mirin
1 heaped teaspoon gochujang
1 tablespoon sweet black vinegar
2 tablespoons dark soy sauce

Place all the ingredients in a large bowl and whisk until
combined.

Transfer to a lidded container or jar and store in the fridge.

spicy cherry hoisin sauce

makes 200ml (7fl oz)

50g (2oz) hoisin sauce
1 tablespoon tamarind paste
1 tablespoon chilli oil
2 heaped tablespoons cocktail
   cherries, finely chopped
2 sprigs of mint, finely chopped
2 tablespoons orange juice

2 tablespoons plum sauce
1cm (½in) piece of ginger,
   finely chopped
2 tablespoons water

Place all the ingredients in a large bowl and whisk really
well so all the components are mixed thoroughly.

Transfer to a lidded container or jar and store in the fridge.

....

citrus ponzu

makes 160ml (5fl oz)

1 tablespoon mirin
1 teaspoon rice vinegar
60ml (2fl oz) soy sauce
1½ tablespoons lime juice
1 teaspoon chilli oil

20ml (⅔fl oz) orange juice
1 teaspoon sesame oil
1 fresh red chilli, finely
   chopped

Place all the ingredients except the chilli in a large bowl
and whisk until combined. Add the chilli and stir.

Transfer to a lidded container and store in the fridge.

miso sesame dressing

makes 100ml (3½fl oz)

100g (3½oz) miso paste
2 teaspoons pickling liquor
 (see page 178)
2 teaspoons sesame oil
1 tablespoon rice vinegar
½ lime, juiced
2 teaspoons sesame seeds

Place all the ingredients except the lime juice and sesame seeds in a container and, using a stick blender, whisk together well.

Add the lime juice and blend again, then add the sesame seeds and mix using a spoon.

Decant into a lidded container or jar and store in the fridge.

shiok marinade

makes 450g (16oz)

100g (3½oz) fresh ginger, roughly chopped (no need to peel)
1 bulb garlic, peeled
1 tablespoon ground turmeric
5 medium-size red chillies, roughly chopped
large bunch of coriander, leaves picked
small bunch of mint, leaves picked
3 medium limes, juiced
150ml (5fl oz) tamari sauce
50ml (2fl oz) vegetable oil

Place all the ingredients in a container and, using a stick blender, blend to a coarse paste.

Decant into a lidded container and store in the fridge.

✷ **Why not make this paste in bulk and freeze in ice-cube trays?**

ginger syrup

makes 100ml (3½fl oz)

25g (1oz) fresh ginger, peeled and cut into large chunks
50g (2oz) caster sugar
100ml (3½fl oz) water

Place all the ingredients in a saucepan and heat to allow the sugar to dissolve. Reduce the heat and simmer for about 20 minutes (the longer you cook it, the more intense the ginger flavour) so the ginger can infuse into the syrup.

Allow to cool, then transfer to a lidded container or jar and store in the fridge.

gyoza sauce

makes 75ml (2½fl oz)

1 small garlic clove, crushed
generous pinch of sea salt
½ red chilli, deseeded and finely chopped
50ml (2fl oz) malt vinegar
1 tablespoon caster sugar
125ml (4fl oz) light soy sauce
1 teaspoon sesame oil

Place the garlic with the salt and chilli in a pestle and mortar and grind together until it forms a paste.

Transfer the paste to a saucepan with the vinegar and sugar and, over a low heat and stirring, simmer gently until the sugar dissolves. Stir in the soy sauce and sesame oil.

Either use immediately or transfer to an airtight container and store in the fridge. It should keep for several weeks.

coconut + ginger sauce

makes 500ml (18fl oz)

1 medium white onion
4 garlic cloves
4cm (20g/¾oz) piece of ginger
4cm (20g/¾oz) piece of
   galangal
25g jalapeno peppers
large bunch of mint (20g/¾oz)
60g (2oz) coriander

50g (2oz) lemongrass
100ml (3½fl oz) vegetable oil
400ml (14oz) tin coconut milk
1 tablespoon (10g/¼oz)
   cornflour
2 large pinches salt
pinch of sugar
juice of 2 large limes

Roughly chop the vegetables and herbs. Smash the lemongrass with the back of a knife and chop. Place these in a food processor and blend into a paste.

Place a thick-bottomed saucepan on a medium heat and add the oil. Once hot, add the paste and cook for 7–9 minutes. Add 100ml (3½fl oz) water and bring to a boil, then add the coconut milk and bring to boil again. Mix cornflour in a little water, making sure there are no lumps, and add this slowly to the sauce, whisking continuously. Add the salt, sugar and lime juice. Remove from the heat and set aside to cool.

chilli men sauce

makes 400ml (14fl oz)

2 medium red onions
4 garlic cloves
4cm (20g/¾oz) piece ginger
6 medium red peppers
20g (¾oz) birds eye chillies
25g (1oz) lemongrass
125ml (4fl oz) vegetable oil

60g (2oz) sriracha sauce
125g (4½oz) tomato ketchup
10ml (2 teaspoons) chilli oil
15g (½oz) sugar
2 large pinches salt
pepper, to taste

Roughly chop the vegetables. Smash the lemongrass with the back of a knife and chop. Place these in a food processor and blend into a paste.

Place a thick-bottomed pan on a low heat and add the oil. Once hot, add the paste and cook on a low heat for 15 minutes. Now add the sriracha, tomato ketchup, chilli oil and 125ml (4fl oz) water and mix. Cook for another 15 minutes, stirring occasionally. You will see oil appearing on the sides of the pan. Add the sugar and salt, and season to taste with pepper. Remove from heat and set aside to cool.

yakitori sauce

makes 125ml (4fl oz)

4 tablespoons light soy sauce
110g (4oz) caster sugar
1 tablespoon dark soy sauce
2 tablespoons sake

Place the light soy sauce and sugar in a small saucepan and gently simmer over a low heat. Stir until the sugar dissolves and then continue to simmer for about 5 minutes until the liquid starts to reduce and thicken.

Add the dark soy and sake, stir and leave to cool. Either use immediately or transfer to an airtight container and store in the fridge. It should keep for several weeks.

amai sauce

makes 275ml (9fl oz)

3 tablespoons caster sugar
1 tablespoon rice vinegar
1 tablespoon malt vinegar
1½ tablespoons tomato ketchup

2 tablespoons tamarind concentrate
1 tablespoon light soy sauce
1 tablespoon dark soy sauce
a pinch of salt

Place the sugar and vinegars in a small saucepan over a medium-low heat and stir until dissolved.

Add the tomato ketchup and tamarind and mix well, then stir in the soy sauces and salt and bring back to the boil. Using a wooden spoon, skim away any impurities that rise to the surface. It might foam a little.

Reduce the heat and simmer for 30 minutes until it becomes a sticky sauce.

firecracker sauce

makes 250ml (9fl oz)

50ml (2fl oz) yakitori sauce (see opposite)

50ml (2fl oz) oyster sauce or vegetarian oyster sauce

100ml (3½fl oz) sriracha sauce

2 tablespoons fish sauce or vegetarian oyster sauce

50ml (2fl oz) vegetable oil

2 tablespoons dried chilli flakes, to taste

6 tablespoons runny honey or 3 tablespoons agave syrup and 3 tablespoons sweet chilli sauce

Place all the ingredients in a small saucepan over a medium-low heat, bring to the boil and then reduce the heat to a simmer.

Cook for about 15–20 minutes until the sauce thickens to a syrup-like consistency. Add more chilli flakes to taste.

Serve instantly or transfer to an airtight jar and keep in the fridge for up to 3 weeks.

katsu curry sauce

serves 2

2–3 tablespoons vegetable oil

1 onion, finely chopped

1 garlic clove, crushed

2.5cm (1in) piece of ginger, peeled and grated

1 teaspoon ground turmeric

2 heaped tablespoons mild curry powder

1 tablespoon plain flour

300ml (10fl oz) chicken or vegetable stock

100ml (3½fl oz) coconut milk

1 teaspoon light soy sauce

1 teaspoon caster sugar, to taste

Place the oil in a saucepan over a medium heat. Add the onion, garlic and ginger and cook until softened. Lower the heat, add the spices and cook for 2–3 minutes.

Add the flour and stir over the heat to cook it out, then slowly add the chicken or vegetable stock. Bring to a simmer and add the coconut milk, soy sauce and sugar, to taste. For a perfectly smooth sauce, pass the mixture through a sieve.

Store in an airtight container in the fridge for up to 3 days.

teriyaki sauce

makes 125ml (4fl oz)

1 tablespoon sake

1 tablespoon mirin

6 tablespoons light soy sauce

1cm (½in) cube fresh ginger

½ garlic clove

1 teaspoon sugar

Place all the ingredients in a small saucepan and gently simmer over a low heat until the sugar has dissolved and the sauce has reduced slightly. Set aside to cool.

✱ **To make spicy teriyaki sauce, mix in a tablespoon of miso paste and a teaspoon of shichimi at the end.**

chilli katsu sauce

makes 125ml (4fl oz)

75ml (3fl oz) sriracha sauce

50ml (2fl oz) sweet chilli sauce

1 teaspoon paprika

2 teaspoons malt vinegar

Place all the ingredients in a bowl or large jar and whisk together until smooth.

Store in an airtight container in the fridge for up to a month.

raisukaree sauce

makes 300ml (10fl oz)

1 tablespoon ground cumin

1 tablespoon ground turmeric

2 garlic cloves, roughly chopped

2.5cm (1in) piece of ginger, roughly chopped

1 lime, juice and zest

a handful of fresh coriander leaves, roughly chopped

1 teaspoon sugar

2 tablespoons soy sauce

1 lemongrass stalk, stem removed and finely sliced

2 spring onions, roughly chopped

1 red chilli, deseeded and finely sliced

1 teaspoon light soy sauce

a pinch of salt

1 teaspoon sugar

2 tablespoons vegetable oil

150ml (5fl oz) vegetable stock

150ml (5fl oz) coconut milk

Heat a wide-based pan over a medium-high heat for 5 minutes. Take off the heat and add the cumin and turmeric, then stir well until fragrant, taking care not to burn the spices. Place all the ingredients except the stock and coconut milk into a blender and blitz until smooth.

Add the curry paste and cook on a medium heat for 10 minutes, then add the vegetable stock and coconut milk. Turn up the heat and bring to the boil. Once boiling, reduce the heat and simmer for 10 minutes.

wagamama dressing

makes 125ml (4fl oz)

2 teaspoons finely chopped shallots

2.5cm (1in) piece of ginger, peeled and grated

1 garlic clove, crushed

1 tablespoon tomato ketchup

1½ tablespoons rice wine vinegar

1 tablespoon water

100ml (3½fl oz) vegetable oil

3 tablespoons light soy sauce

A true favourite which has stood the test of time.

Place all the ingredients in a bowl or large jar and whisk together until smooth.

Store in an airtight container in the fridge for up to 3 days.

sticky white or brown rice

makes 400g (14oz) cooked rice

200g (7oz) raw rice

Wash the rice twice, and place in a pan with 400ml (14fl oz) water. Bring to the boil and then turn right down and simmer for 12–14 minutes. You may need to add a dash more water for your brown rice.

✱ Rice doubles in weight when cooked, so use half the amount of raw rice to make the amount of cooked rice you require.

pickling liquor

makes 100ml (3½fl oz)

100ml (3½fl oz) rice vinegar

juice of ½ lime

1 tablespoon caster sugar

pinch of sea salt

Place a saucepan over a low heat and all the pickling liquor ingredients with 3 tablespoons of water. Heat and stir until the sugar and salt have dissolved, then adjust the flavouring to taste. Transfer to a large, heatproof bowl or jar and set aside to cool.

spicy vinegar

makes 150ml (5fl oz)

50g (2oz) caster sugar

2 tablespoons water

5 tablespoons malt vinegar

5 tablespoons light soy sauce

a pinch of sea salt

½ red chilli, deseeded and finely chopped

3 sprigs of coriander, stalks removed and leaves finely chopped

Place the sugar and water in a small saucepan over a medium-low heat and stir until dissolved. Remove from the heat and add the vinegar, soy sauce and a pinch of salt. Store in an airtight container in the fridge for up to 4 weeks and stir in the chilli and coriander just before use.

vegan kimchee

This classic Korean dish accompaniment is made by fermenting cabbage and carrots in a flavoursome sauce, pungent with garlic and spice. Kimchee adds flavour to many Asian dishes.

makes 1 jar

1 Chinese cabbage, washed

2 carrots, peeled and cut into matchsticks or coarsely grated

60g (2oz) coarse sea salt

½ daikon or 8 salad radishes, coarsely grated

4 spring onions, finely sliced

kimchee paste

3 garlic cloves, crushed

2.5cm (1in) piece of ginger, peeled and grated

1 tablespoon tamari sauce

1 tablespoon miso paste

2 tablespoons gochujang or sriracha

1 tablespoon golden caster sugar

3 tablespoons rice vinegar

Slice the cabbage lengthways into four and remove the core from each piece. Place in a large bowl with the carrots and cover with the salt, ensuring the vegetables are well coated. Cover with water and set aside to brine for up to 2 hours.

To make the kimchee paste, place the garlic, ginger, tamari sauce, miso paste, gochujang or sriracha, sugar and rice vinegar together in a small bowl and stir to blend.

Once the cabbage and carrot mixture is ready, drain and rinse under cold running water to remove any salt crystals.

Return the cabbage mixture to the large bowl and stir through the paste, along with the daikon and spring onions. Serve straight away or pack tightly into a large sterilised jar, seal and leave at room temperature to ferment overnight or for up to 72 hours.

While fermenting, insert a clean chopstick or butter knife every now and then to release any air bubbles. You can also add some additional brine to keep all the vegetables submerged if necessary.

A sealed jar of kimchee will keep in the fridge for up to 4 weeks. The flavour will improve the longer it's left.

hirata
steamed buns

Hirata are traditional Japanese steamed buns, otherwise known as 'bao' in China. They are delicious pillows of soft dough and while they do take some time to prepare, they are worth the effort.

makes 18 buns

525g (18½oz) plain flour, plus extra for dusting
1½ tablespoons caster sugar, plus a pinch
½ teaspoon sea salt
1 teaspoon fast-action dried yeast
50ml (2fl oz) milk (or plant-based milk)
1 tablespoon sunflower oil, plus extra for brushing
1 tablespoon rice wine vinegar
1 teaspoon baking powder

Place the flour, sugar and salt in a large mixing bowl and stir to combine.

Dissolve the yeast with a pinch of sugar in 1 tablespoon of warm water, then add to the flour with the milk, sunflower oil, rice wine vinegar and 200ml (7fl oz) tepid water. Using your hands, mix to form a dough, adding more tepid water if necessary.

Dust a clean work surface with flour and knead the dough for up to 15 minutes, until smooth, then place in a bowl and cover with a damp cloth. Set aside to rise until doubled in size – this can take up to 2 hours.

Once risen, tip the dough out onto a clean floured work surface and punch the centre. Using your hands, flatten out the dough and sprinkle with the baking powder, then knead for a final 5 minutes.

Using your hands, roll the dough into a long 3cm (1¼in) thick sausage shape, then slice into 3cm (1¼in) thick rounds, to make 18 rounds in total.

Using your hands, roll each piece of dough into a ball and leave to rest for 3 minutes.

Using a rolling pin, flatten each ball into an oval shape about 4mm (¼in) thick. Brush the surface of each oval of dough with a little oil, and also oil the length of a chopstick.

Place the chopstick in the centre of each oval of dough and fold the dough over the chopstick. Carefully slide away the oiled chopstick.

Cut out 18 squares of parchment paper and arrange on a baking tray. Place a bun on each piece of paper, cover with lightly oiled clingfilm or a clean tea towel and set aside to prove in a warm place for around 1½ hours, until doubled in size.

Place a large steamer over a medium-high heat and steam the buns in batches for about 8 minutes, until risen and fluffy.

gyoza skins

Ready-made gyoza skins are available in most Asian supermarkets, but why not have a go at making your own from scratch. The process is mindful and rewarding.

makes 35-40 skins

240g (9oz) strong white flour
½ teaspoon salt
120ml (4fl oz) water, just boiled
cornflour, for dusting
2–3 tablespoons vegetable oil

Sift the flour into a large mixing bowl. In another bowl, add the salt to the just-boiled water and mix until dissolved. Add the water to the flour little by little, stirring with chopsticks or a spatula as you go. Once the flour and water have started to combine, use your hands to form the dough into a ball. If too dry, add an extra ½ tablespoon of water at a time.

Transfer the dough to a floured work surface and knead for up to 10 minutes until the texture is smooth and elastic. Cut the dough ball in half and roll each piece into a log, approximately 4cm (1½in) in diameter. Wrap each log in clingfilm and set aside to rest for 30 minutes.

Once rested, unwrap the dough, sprinkle some cornflour onto your work surface and slice each log into approximately 12 pieces. Arrange these on a large plate and cover with a clean damp towel to prevent the dough from drying out. Using your hands, roll each piece of dough into a ball and then press flat. Next, using a rolling pin, roll the dough (turning 90 degrees after every roll) to create a thin, round circle that is approximately 8–9cm (3–3½in) in diameter.

Using an 8cm (3in) cookie cutter, press down onto the dough to cut out a perfect circle, then transfer to a plate and dust lightly with cornflour to prevent the skins from sticking together as they accumulate. Re-roll the scraps to create additional skins. Cover the wrappers with damp kitchen towel whilst making the gyozas. Or, if not using immediately, cover with clingfilm and keep in the fridge for 3–4 days, or in the freezer for up to a month.

When you are ready to fill the gyoza, take a heaped teaspoon of filling and place it in the centre of each piece of dough. Fold one side over to encase the filling and bring the edges together, pinching them to seal. Finally, pleat the edges together.

Heat the oil in a large non-stick frying pan. Once hot and working in batches so as not to overcrowd the pan, add the gyozas and cook for 3–4 minutes until the underside turns golden brown. Once browned, add 60ml (2fl oz) water to the pan and cover with a lid. Steam for 3 minutes, then remove the lid and cook off the excess water. Add 1 tablespoon oil and continue to cook until the other side of the gyzoa has crisped and turned brown. Once completely cooked, plate immediately and serve with our gyoza dipping sauce (see page 173).

index

Plain flour / all-purpose flour
Self-raising flour / self-rising flour
Bicarbonate of soda / baking soda
Caster sugar / superfine sugar
Icing sugar / confectioner's sugar
Cornflour / cornstarch

Aubergine / eggplant
Courgette / zucchini
Spring onions / scallions
Coriander (fresh) / cilantro
Longstem broccoli / broccolini
Red/green pepper / bell pepper
Soya beans / soy beans
Pomegranate seeds / pomegranate arils
Prawns / shrimps
Mangetout / snow peas
Pak choi / bok choy
Desiccated coconut / shredded coconut
Chilli flakes / red pepper flakes

Kitchen paper / paper towels
Frying pan / skillet
Griddle pan / grill pan

acknowledgements

wagamama your way is a result of the collective passion and hard work of some very special people.

They know who they are, but I would personally like to thank them for helping to create a cookbook that we at wagamama are all so proud of…

To Eleanor Hardy and Surendra Yeiju, for helping me fill the pages of this cookbook with so many fresh and exciting new recipes.

To Howard Shooter and Rose Mordaunt for capturing a book full of beautiful photos that bring the essence of wagamama to life.

To Denise Smart, our fabulous food stylist, for making the food look exceptional every time.

To Charlie Hiscocks, our committed navigator, for keeping us on the right path.

To Emma Woods, for bringing the idea of this book to life, and to Thomas Heier for his unwavering support.

To Kay Bartlett, Aisling Lithgow, Kelly Lithgow and Sarah Sammons (from our marketing team), for living and breathing wagamama.

Our development team, Jamie Henderson, Muthu Krishnan, Nabish Rai and Karl Thompson, for your loyal dedication to our fresh food philosophy.

And of course, thank you to all of the head chefs, general managers and teams within our restaurants who are the heart and soul of wagamama.

An Hachette UK Company
www.hachette.co.uk

First published in Great Britain in 2021 by
Kyle Books, an imprint of Octopus Publishing Group Limited
Carmelite House
50 Victoria Embankment
London EC4Y 0DZ

www.kylebooks.co.uk
www.octopusbooksusa.com

ISBN: 9780857837196
ISBN: 9781914239182 Waterstones Exclusive Edition

Distributed in the US by Hachette Book Group, 1290 Avenue
of the Americas, 4th and 5th Floors, New York, NY 10104

Distributed in Canada by Canadian Manda Group, 664 Annette St.,
Toronto, Ontario, Canada M6S 2C8

Publisher: Joanna Copestick
Publishing Director: Judith Hannam
Designer: Paul Palmer-Edwards
Photographer: Howard Shooter
Food styling: Denise Smart
Props styling: Wei Tang
Production: Allison Gonsalves

A Cataloguing in Publication record for this title
is available from the British Library

Printed and bound in Italy

10 9 8 7 6 5 4 3 2 1

Also published by Kyle Books